CHELTENHAM
HERITAGE WALKS

DAVID ELDER

AMBERLEY

For my Mother

First published 2014

Amberley Publishing
The Hill, Stroud
Gloucestershire, GL5 4EP

www.amberley-books.com

British Library Cataloguing in Publication Data.
A catalogue record for this book is available from the British Library.

ISBN 978 1 4456 2243 9 (paperback)
ISBN 978 1 4456 2266 8 (ebook)

Typesetting and Origination by Amberley Publishing.
Printed in Great Britain.

Contents

Major Heritage Locations in Cheltenham Town Centre

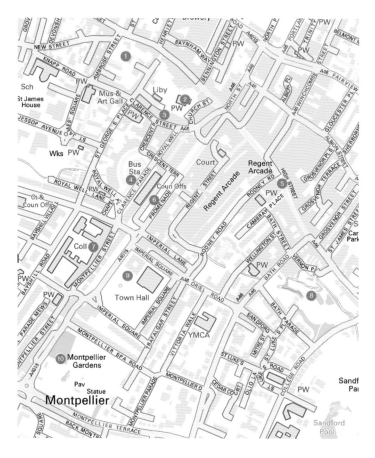

1. Jenner Gardens (including Cheltenham Chapel)
2. Cheltenham Minster (St Mary's)
3. The Wilson, Cheltenham's Art Gallery & Museum
4. The Royal Crescent
5. High Street (including former sites of The Plough Hotel and the Assembly Rooms)
6. The Promenade (including the Neptune Fountain and statue of Edward Wilson)

7. Cheltenham Ladies' College
8. Sandford Park (including Barrett's Mill)
9. Imperial Gardens (including the Town Hall and statue of Gustav Holst)
10. Montpellier Gardens (including the nearby Rotunda and caryatids)

Introduction

Often the best way to explore a place is on foot: '… any morning, we can set out, with the least possible baggage, and discover the world' writes Thomas A. Clark in his enduring prose poem, 'In Praise of Walking' (2000). 'Walking is the human way of getting about. Always, everywhere, people have walked,' he notes, adding later, 'There are things we will never see, unless we walk to them.' How true this is of Cheltenham, a town so richly steeped in cultural heritage. While many of Cheltenham's delights are easily won, well signposted or appear centre stage, equally many of its secrets lie hidden or undiscovered in alleyways, on the edges of pedestrianised zones or buried beneath buildings and sites which have undergone sometimes repeated redevelopment. After all, Cheltenham has never been stuck in a time warp; it has constantly reinvented itself through the ages, from a medieval village served by a few mills, to a fashionable inland resort to which the rich and famous once flocked to take the spa waters and enjoy walks, rides and social events, right up to the present day, where much of its appeal is celebrated through its festivals of music, literature and horse racing, its world-class schools and colleges and, of course, its Regency architecture.

This book of informative walks is aimed at visitors and residents alike, with the intention of helping you to become better acquainted with Cheltenham's historical and cultural heritage, particularly through the people who have observed the town, been inspired by it, or helped to shape it in some way. The order in which the walks appear has been chosen with a general chronological sequence in mind, starting with Cheltenham's medieval mills and finishing with some of the town's recently acquired contemporary art installations. However, the ordering is very approximate, since each walk spans a variety of different historical periods. Each is a separate, self-contained walk based around a specific theme. Therefore, there is no need to follow the suggested sequence in order to enjoy each one; where necessary, however, relevant cross references are used to provide important links between the walks. While small summary maps of the walks are provided, it is also recommended that you bring with you a detailed street atlas of the town, which is obtainable from any of the local bookshops.

The walks cover the following main themes:

Walk 1: By the Waters of Cheltenham. Explores the River Chelt, making a journey from medieval times, when a number of mills formed the basis of the town's economy, to the present day, where the river shows the challenge caused by potentially devastating floods.

Walk 2: In Search of Health and Inland Waters. Explores the spa town's numerous wells, some of which are still present, while others are today lost, hidden or forgotten.

Walk 3: From Elysium to Hell. Explores the places of Cheltenham's rich literary heritage, including sites associated with writers such as Tennyson and W.H. Davies.

Walk 4: Spiritual Advantages. Celebrates many of the town's landmarks that have inspired different religious faiths and beliefs.

Walk 5: Through the Looking Glass. Explores many of the sites associated with the writers and poets who have created Charlton Kings' rich literary heritage.

Walk 6: Cheltenham in Antarctica. Explores Cheltenham's connections with Antarctic exploration, principally through one of its most famous sons, Edward Wilson (1872–1912), who perished with Captain Scott at the South Pole.

Walk 7: From *Lansdown Castle* to *Egdon Heath*. Celebrates the sites in the town which are associated with the life and music of Cheltenham-born composer Gustav Holst (1874–1934).

Walk 8: Tree and Street. Provides a tour along the town's finest tree-lined roads and parks and gardens, providing a unique perspective on its historical and literary heritage.

Walk 9: Theme and Variations. Explores Cheltenham's rich artistic heritage.

For anyone requiring a quick introductory tour of some of Cheltenham's major heritage sites, the map on page 4 may be used to navigate between key points of interest which are never more than a ten-minute walk from The Promenade.

   The Promenade, laid out in 1818 as Cheltenham's most fashionable thoroughfare, also contains two prominent features: the **Neptune Fountain**, the design of which was based on the Trevi Fountain in Rome, and, next to it, the **statue of Edward Wilson**, which was sculpted by Lady Kathleen Scott, widow of Captain Scott. Just around the corner from here, in St George's Road, is the world-famous **Cheltenham Ladies' College**. Although the present group of buildings, part of which now covers the site of Cheltenham's original spa, only dates back to 1873, the original building was opened twenty years earlier, located on the site where Cambray Court flats now stand. Returning to The Promenade, walking towards the Montpellier area, on your left you'll see the **Imperial Square and Gardens**, often referred to as 'the jewel in Cheltenham's crown'. Dominating the square is the Edwardian Baroque **Town Hall**, which was built in 1902–3 and where the Central Spa used to be located. In fact, you can sometimes still taste the spa water in the lobby here. Behind the Town Hall was the site of the Winter Gardens, Cheltenham's 'Crystal Palace'. Built in 1878 as a venue for various concerts, performances and events, it was demolished at the beginning of the Second World War. Despite this, there are still visible signs of its former existence through the layout of the paths in the ornamental gardens, which align with the position of the Winter Gardens' entrances. The gardens are also the location for the **Gustav Holst statue**, which was unveiled in 2008 to celebrate the composer of *The Planets*. Continuing towards Montpellier, on your left you'll see **Montpellier Gardens**, which were developed shortly after the opening of Montpellier Spa in 1809, being originally conceived as exclusive pleasure gardens for visitors to the spa. On your right, along Montpellier Walk, you'll see the thirty-two **caryatids**. These figures of 'armless ladies', two of which date from 1840, act as supporting columns for the lintels of shop façades. A little farther on is the **Rotunda** building, now a Lloyds bank, where the Montpellier Spa was developed by Henry Thompson in 1809. An alternative tour starting from The Promenade is to walk to **Royal Crescent**, one of the oldest Regency buildings in Cheltenham, which was originally developed in 1806–10 to provide accommodation for visitors to the spa. From here there is a circular route which may be followed: firstly visit **The Wilson**, Cheltenham's Art Gallery & Museum, then incorporate **Jenner Gardens**, which includes Cheltenham Chapel, built in 1809 and once used for vaccination clinics by Dr Edward Jenner, before visiting **Cheltenham Minster,** formerly **St Mary's**, which dates back to the twelfth century, and then head up the **High Street**, first paved in 1787 where, at the Regent Arcade entrance, you'll see the former site of The Plough Hotel and, at the Lloyds bank, the former site of the Assembly Rooms. Continuing on towards **Sandford Park** you'll find the town's main mill at Cambray, now known as Barrett's Mill, from where the River Chelt was once diverted from the millpond to flow down the centre of the High Street in order to cleanse it. The circular route back to The Promenade may be completed by walking along Bath Road and then Imperial Square.

Walk 1

By the Waters of Cheltenham

Distance: 3.25 miles (1.25 miles if only first section included)

Minimum Time: 1 hour 50 mins (1 hour if only first section included)

Parking: Bath Parade car park is the most convenient.

Where to Eat and Drink: In the first section of the walk The Restoration Inn, which is located at 55–57 High Street and is reputed to be Cheltenham's oldest pub, or Café Moochoo, at 51 High Street. In the second section the Bayshill at 85 St George's Place and the Waitrose café are the most convenient.

Where to stay: The Abbey Hotel at 14–16 Bath Parade (Tel. 01242 516053, www.abbeyhotel-cheltenham.com) is conveniently close to the start of the walk.

The Neptune Fountain.

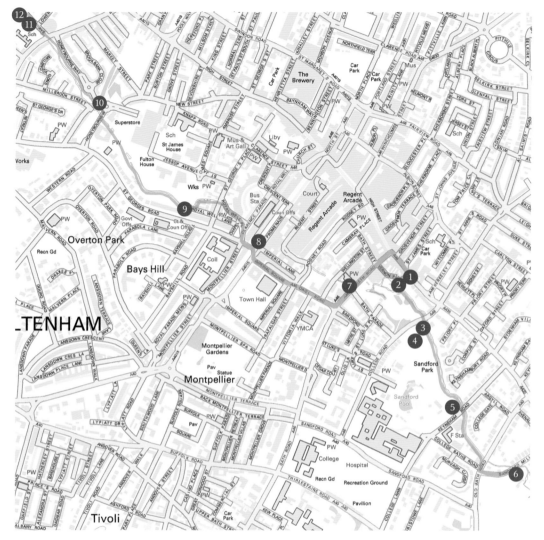

1. Stone bridge next to Barrett's Mill
2. Barrett's Mill
3. Surviving parts of Chalybeate Spa
4. *The Weathered Man*
5. Public drinking fountain
6. Sandford Mill
7. Site of Wellington Mansion
8. Neptune Fountain
9. Site of cold bath
10. Site of Upper Alstone Mill
11. Lower Alstone Mill
12. Alstone House

'By the waters of Cheltenham,' wrote Lord Byron, 'I sat down and drank, when I remembered thee oh Georgiana Cottage! As for our harps, we hanged them up upon the willows that grew thereby.' After ending his passionate affair with Lady Caroline Lamb, Byron came to Cheltenham to take advantage of the spa waters because they were 'very medicinal, and sufficiently disgusting'. Byron stayed at Georgiana Cottage, a Regency building originally named after Georgiana, Duchess of Devonshire, who visited Cheltenham in 1780. Sadly, the building, which once stood on the corner of Bath Street, was demolished in 1928. However, by visiting the stretch of the River Chelt which flows along the former site of Wellington Mansion (see below), one can imagine the place to which Byron refers, since it was here where the willows once grew 'thereby', along the side of the river in a continuous line.

The name of the river is a back-formation from the place name, which probably comes from either Celta's Hamm, or 'an enclosure or river meadow by a hill-slope called Celte' (in Old English). It flows from its source in the hills above Dowdeswell in the south-east to join the Severn at Wainlodes Hill to the west. For much of its course through the centre of town the river is invisible, hidden from view behind fences and banks, underground or in open culverts. This walk is divided into two sections. However, if you walk along either you will be making a journey from medieval times to the present day. You will see a number of mills (now disused or adapted) which formed the basis of the town's economy, and elements of the town's recently installed flood defence systems, built following the devastating flood in 2007, in which Cheltenham Borough Council incurred an estimated £8.8 million in costs through loss of income, additional staffing and other emergency costs. Together the walk's two sections follow the course of the river (one way) for approximately 1.5 miles.

🐾 **The walk starts at Bath Parade car park. Turn right from the car park into Bath Road.**
Walk past the entrance to Sandford Park, which you will visit later.
🐾 **Turn right into the High Street.**
There are several places to stop here for food or drink, including the Restoration Inn or Café Moochoo.
🐾 **Turn right into Barrat's Mill Lane. Cross over a brick bridge (1).**

★ Washington Irving

Although this is unlikely to be the bridge in question, in 1820 Washington Irving wrote that while he was returning from a walk to the spas, he crossed by 'a fairy little bridge, a gurgling sporting rivulet scarcely two yards over, the beauty of which [he] had several times previously remarked'. When he inquired about the name of 'that pretty brook', he was told 'with a countenance of mingled surprise and concern' that it was not a brook but the River Chelt. Following this, Irving half expected 'to see the indignant spirit of the stream, bending in misty semblance on the view, prepared to assert its honour, and avenge the affront'.

🐾 **On your right you will see Barrett's Mill (2), now a private house and previously known as Cheltenham or Cambray Mill.**

★ Barrett's Mill

The Domesday Book of 1086 described Cheltenham as having two old Saxon mills owned by King Edward 'rendering 11s 3d'. Although neither was named, it is generally assumed that one of the two original mills was at Cambray. Through the ages it has been known both as Cheltenham Mill and Barrett's Mill after the name of one of its owners. From the 1500s, it was the custom for the river to be diverted from the millpond to flow down the centre of the High Street in order to cleanse it. Whenever this happened, pedestrians used stepping stones to cross the street. By 1786 improvements were made by cutting a new road through the town with a channel on either side for the water. However, in 1807 a dispute arose concerning the town's right to use the water from the mill. The then miller, William Humphris Barrett, fearful of claims for damages, repeatedly refused to stop the flow of water to other mills further downstream. Eventually the problem was resolved through the formation of a water company

View of Barrett's Mill.

and then, in the 1870s, by the council's decision to purchase the mill so that the river levels could be lowered to help with flood prevention. Nevertheless, as one of Cheltenham's most colourful characters in its history, Barrett's name still lives on, albeit misspelt, in Barrat's Mill Lane.

🦶 **Follow the path round to the right which takes you to the far side of the mill pond.**

A large millstone is located here. Notice along the way the landscaped area below the side of the mill. Although these rockeries and rivulets were designed as part of the inauguration of Sandford Park in 1927, old maps reveal that this area was laid out along similar lines as part of the original mill complex. This suggests that there were two forks to the river, which then merged again before rejoining the main river, which now meanders before going underground to cross Bath Road.

🦶 **Return to the brick bridge. Turn right in front of it to follow the footpath along the river.**

Notice the attractive Unwin fountain (see walk 8) on your right.

🦶 **Cross over College Road.**

Immediately on your right you can see the surviving parts of the Chalybeate Spa (**3**), which are now being used as a building for a volunteer centre and the Parks Department.

★ Chalybeate Spa

One of Cheltenham's early and now forgotten spas, the Chalybeate Spa, was opened in 1801 by the miller William Humphris Barrett at the start of the town's rapid rise as a watering resort following King George III's visit. When a rival Chalybeate Spa opened at Fowler's Cottage in Cambray Place six years later (see walk 2), it was renamed the Original Chalybeate Spa. With its iron- and mineral-rich waters it soon became a popular alternative to the predominantly saline waters of the Old Well, and its reputation was further enhanced through personal endorsement from the politician Sir Francis Burdett (1770–1844). Medical opinion of the day claimed that its waters were suitable for treating eye complaints, convulsions, nervous disorders and even female infertility. During the 1820s it was at the centre of a bitter dispute between Barrett and the town's paving commissioners, who wished to build a new road to provide access to the spa from the High Street rather than rely on the existing footpath from Barrett's Mill. However, the mill owner was not to be persuaded, and so a state of stalemate ensued until the land changed ownership in 1842 when College Road was built. However, it made no difference to the spa itself, which closed during the following decade.

👣 **Continue for a short distance past the building with the river on your left.**
On your right, in the main section of grass, you'll see the statue known as *The Weathered Man* (**4**).

★ The Weathered Man
The statue was installed in 2006 and adorns a £4 million drainage culvert in Sandford Park which, as part of Cheltenham's £21 million flood relief project, was designed to protect the town from a once-in-100-years flood. It was created by local sculptor James Gould, who designed it as a 'relaxing' feature, his inspiration coming from a family photo which showed him lying on a bridge and looking down at water below. However, so far it has had a rather chequered history, on the one hand being viewed as a waste of money by some local residents and, on the other, being the target for theft – in September 2010 two men attempted to steal the bronze statue, which weighs half a tonne.

👣 **Continue along the riverside path.**
Notice the curious stone ornamental structure just before the Keynsham Road entrance to the park. This was a public drinking fountain (**5**) of Gothic Revival style which was originally commissioned in 1891.

The Weathered Man, which covers a drainage culvert.

The curious stone ornamental structure, which originally functioned as a drinking fountain.

★ **Public Drinking Fountain**

It was donated for the poor by Victorian benefactors and was originally placed at Westal Green near Lansdown Road. It was moved to its present location in 1929, but no longer functions as a fountain.

👣 **Exit Sandford Park. Head left for 10 metres and then immediately right to continue along the riverside path to Old Bath Road.**

Notice the point at which the river flows under the road. This site, once known as Sandford Bridge, was an important landmark and crossing place in previous centuries.

👣 **Cross over and turn right into Old Bath Road. Then turn left into Sandford Mill Road.**

At No. 40 you'll see Sandford Mill (**6**), which is private property. It's set back from the road and has a millstone outside the front.

★ **Sandford Mill**

For hundreds of years, certainly between the medieval period and the end of the nineteenth century, it operated as one of Cheltenham's most important corn mills. In 1929 the mill machinery was sold, by which time Sandford Mill had become a farm. The mill became derelict from the 1950s before it was restored and converted into a private house during the 1980s.

👣 Retrace your steps back to Barrett's Mill.

Before reaching the mill follow the path round to the left and then right at the *Friendship Circle* (see walk 9).

👣 Exit the park via Bath Road. Turn left to return to Bath Parade car park.

The second section of this walk will allow you to follow the river's course to another disused mill at the west end of the town. This walk will also allow you to see some more of the culverting of the river and sites of earlier features of the town's spa heyday.

👣 To continue the walk cross Bath Road and turn left as far as the Salvation Army community church.

To the left of the church you can observe the straight line of the river. This may appear to be slightly unnatural and, in fact, it is: Colonel Riddell, the wealthy resident of a now demolished house called Wellington Mansion (**7**), which once stood on Bath Road to the left of the river, was interested in having the river flow through the middle of his garden, and so he had its course changed.

★ Wellington Mansion

The single stone pillar and a short section of old railings topped with attractive finials with a Greek anthemion design, which still exist to the left of the river, are the only tangible clues to the grandeur of Colonel Riddell's property, so named because the Duke of Wellington stayed here on two occasions.

🐾 Continue along Bath Road, and then turn right into Oriel Road.

Notice the Playhouse Theatre (see walk 2) on your right, which was once home to Montpellier Baths and, before that, a salts manufactory.

🐾 Turn right into The Promenade where you'll see the Neptune Fountain (8) on your left.

★ Neptune Fountain

The Neptune Fountain (see also walk 9) was constructed in 1893 and shows Neptune being drawn by seahorses. Its water comes from the River Chelt, which lies directly underneath.

🐾 Leave The Promenade by turning right into St George's Road and right again into Clarence Parade. Then turn left into Royal Well Place. Cross over St George's Place and enter the lane to the left of the Bayshill, where you can stop for a drink.

Here you will meet the river again as it emerges from an underground culvert. Around this stretch of the river was the location of a cold bath (9), with facilities for warm bathing too. This was run by a Miss Stapleton as early as 1763 and offered medicinal baths, which were sometimes recommended by physicians as a supplement to drinking the waters. This bath became disused by 1783, while other bathing establishments were later set up in the High Street and in Bath Road.

🐾 Continue along the riverside walkway, keeping the river on your left.

The river then curves round into another culverted section where some of the flood defences can be seen. You will see a Waitrose supermarket on your right.

🐾 You can stop here for food or drink at the Waitrose café.

🐾 After you pass Waitrose walk up a ramp on the right to Honeybourne Way. Cross the road and head downhill towards the roundabout beside Waitrose.

Before heading towards the roundabout there is an option for a slight detour to take in the excellent view of the river and the artisan houses clustered in this area from the white pedestrian bridge.

★ Upper Alstone Mill

It was near here, on the other side of the river, at the junction of Millbrook Street with Great Western Terrace, that Upper Alstone Mill was located (10). Situated close to an increasingly industrialised environment during Victorian times, the mill benefited from an expanded population following the arrival of the railway. By 1870 its owner combined the milling business with running a bakery in the High Street. However, by the early twentieth century it had become a sawmill, following the increasing obsolescence of grist mills and the difficulties faced by local mills in keeping up with the increased demand for flour as Cheltenham's population expanded. In later years, the mill was converted to steam power as a means of supplementing reduced water power, but by the 1920s it was a viable concern and closed, being demolished in the late 1940s. All that remains is the local weir, but even this has been dramatically altered following the development of the Waitrose supermarket site.

🐾 Follow the river along the walkway (river on your left). At the end you will need to rejoin the pavement and, at the end of the road, cross Gloucester Road (pedestrian lights). On the opposite side, turn left and immediately right into Arle Avenue.

Notice that the street on your right is still named Lower Mill Street.

🐾 Keeping the river on your left continue until you reach a modern bridge.

★ Lower Alstone Mill

Here you'll see the building that was originally Lower Alstone Mill (**11**). Today, although the building is not currently being used, it served, until recently, as a social club for the local gasworks. Across the road from this building is a magnificent Queen Anne-period house called Alstone House (**12**), which was built in about 1700 as a residence for Richard Hyett, gentleman.

🐾 Retrace your steps to finish the walk back at Bath Parade car park.

Alstone House, a magnificent Queen Anne-period house.

Walk 2

In Search of Health and Inland Waters

Distance: 4 miles, but the walk may be reduced to 1.9 miles if the extension to Pittville is not included.

Minimum Time: 2 hours 15 mins (or 1 hour 10 mins if only town centre section included).

Parking: Chester Walk (nearest) or Cheltenham Walk (located near Jessop Avenue). There is free parking at Pittville.

Where to Eat and Drink: At start/end of walk Cheltenham Dandy café and Well Walk Tea Room, both in Well Walk, serve snacks and lunches, or you can visit the café at the Wilson Art Gallery & Museum in Clarence Street. In Montpellier, Coffee & Co. at 7 Montpellier Terrace is well worth a visit and also provides superb views of the Rotunda, the site of Montpellier Spa. At Pittville the outdoor café in Central Cross Drive provides snacks and is located on the site of a former spa.

Where to stay: At the Queen's Hotel (Tel. 0118 971 4700, www.queenshotelcheltenham.com) you can stay at the original site of the Sherborne/Imperial Spa. In Bayshill Road the Montpellier Chapter (Tel. 01242 527788, www.themontpellierchapterhotel.com) offers modern spa treatments and is located in the heart of Cheltenham's historic spa area.

The Rotunda building, formerly Montpellier Spa.

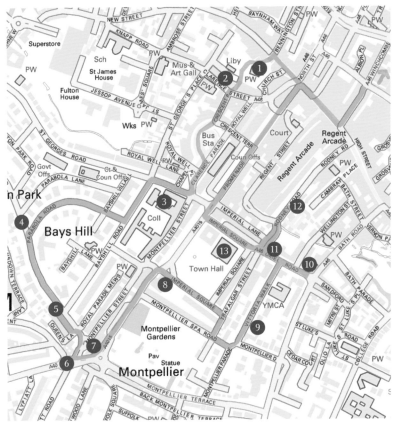

Continuation of walk to sites 14, 15 and 16 on page 23.

1. Cheltenham Minster
2. St Matthew's church
3. Cheltenham Ladies' College
4. Sidney Lodge
5. Royston

6. Gordon Lamp
7. Rotunda
8. Queen's Hotel
9. Vittoria House
10. The Playhouse Theatre

11. Rodney Road car park
12. Site of first Cambray Spa
13. Town Hall

In 1969, nearly two centuries after King George III visited the town and made it famous as a fashionable spa, John Betjeman penned the following lines for a TV series which explored Britain from a helicopter: 'Quality sent its sons and daughters / In search of health to inland waters / To Roman Bath or Cheltenham Spa, / Where the Chalybeate fountains are.' This walk explores the town's numerous wells, some of which are still present, while others today are lost, hidden or forgotten.

In its heyday as a spa between 1790 and the 1830s, Cheltenham was so popular that it even rivalled Bath. Following King George III's visit in 1788, a London newspaper commented that all the fashions became 'completely Cheltenhamised'. The king's visit was described first hand both by the milkmaid poet Ann Yearsley and the diarist and novelist Fanny Burney, who accompanied the royal party as lady-in-waiting to Queen Charlotte. Through its centre of gravity as one of the most favoured of watering places, the town also attracted famous writers, including Lord Byron, who in 1812 wrote, 'I have been here for some time drinking the waters, simply because there are waters to drink, and they are very medicinal, and sufficiently disgusting,' as well as Elizabeth Barrett Browning, Sir Walter Scott, Ireland's national poet

Thomas Moore, and Jane Austen, who visited for three weeks and was aggrieved to hear that her sister was charged three guineas a week for her lodging and accused the landlady of charging for 'the name of the High Street'.

★ **Cheltenham Minster (St Mary's)**

This walk starts at Cheltenham's medieval parish church of St Mary's, now Cheltenham Minster **(1)**. Inside you'll find an extraordinary memorial to Henry Skillicorne, a Manx sea captain who developed Cheltenham's first spa. Reputed to be the longest memorial in the country, it provides a summary of his life and achievements, the final section providing insight into his character: 'He was of great Regularity & Probity, & so temperate as never to have been once intoxicated. Religious without Hypocrisy, Grave without Austerity, of a Cheerful Conversation without Levity, A kind Husband and tender Father. Tall, erect, robust, and active. From an Ill treated Wound while a

The memorial to Henry Skillicorne, Cheltenham Minster.

Prisoner, after an Engagement at Sea, He became a strict Valetudinarian. He lived and dyed an honest man.' Another memorial commemorates Hannah Forty, one of the well's first pumpers. The latter's inscription reads, 'She became pumper at the Old Well in this town on the 12th day of Sep. 1772, and continued in that situation until the 1st day of Jany., 1816, discharging for more than forty three years the duties of her office with credit to herself, and to the satisfaction of the numerous visitors, who during that long period resorted to the Original Spring. A few of those to whom for several seasons she had dispensed the blessings of health, have felt a satisfaction in erecting this memorial to her long and meritorious service.'

🐾 **Leave the church to enter Well Walk.**

This is all that's left now of a once extensive avenue lined with elms and limes that linked the centre of the town to the site of the original spa, today located within the Ladies' College.

🐾 **Cross Clarence Street into Crescent Place.**

Notice St Matthew's church **(2)** on the right, which is located on the site of The Great House. Originally built in 1739 as a private house, The Great House later became the town's principal boarding house, counting George Frederick Handel and Samuel Johnson among some of its most notable visitors.

🐾 **Continue to the end of Crescent Place and proceed through the Royal Crescent.**

Originally part of Church Meadow, this development was built in 1806–10 to provide accommodation for visitors to the spa, and now ranks as one of the oldest Regency buildings in Cheltenham.

🐾 **Proceed to the end of Royal Well Road and turn right into St George's Road.**

This has many fine terraces, including the one on your immediate right which includes the first house where Cheltenham College began in 1841.

🐾 **Cross over towards Cheltenham Ladies' College (3) and turn left into Bayshill Road.**
The entrance of the college is on your left. Here on the right-hand side of the steps you'll see a green Civic Society plaque that commemorates King George III's visit to the Old Well. It reads, 'Here was a pathway to the Old Well where King George took the waters in 1788. It was situated near the Princess Hall.'

★ Old Well
It was on the site of the Ladies' College that the story of Cheltenham Spa began. The Old (or Original) Well was officially discovered in 1716 by William Mason, a local farmer, who noticed pigeons pecking at salt deposits in his field. Its popularity as a healing well soon prompted Mason to charge local residents for its use. However, it was not systematically developed until it was taken over by Mason's son-in-law, Henry Skillicorne, who built a pump room in 1738. The saline and mildly chalybeate water was recommended by doctors as a cure for virtually everything, particularly for leg ulcers, bowel complaints and 'female diseases'. Its fortunes peaked during King George III's five-week visit, and it was renamed the Royal (or King's) Well. However, by the time the Ladies' College took over the site for development in 1873 its popularity had waned due to competition from rival wells. The well now lies buried beneath the college's Princess Hall.

🐾 **Turn right into Parabola Road. Walk to the end and turn right into Overton Road.**
Proceed for 100 metres and on your left you'll find Sidney Lodge, the site of Fauconberg Lodge (4).

★ Fauconberg Lodge
Also known as Bayshill House, Fauconberg Lodge was the grand residence located on the brow of the hill that was lent by Lord Fauconberg to accommodate the king and the royal entourage. Fanny Burney, the queen's lady-in-waiting, recorded in her diary that it was 'situated on a most sweet spot, surrounded with lofty hills beautifully variegated, and bounded, for the principal object, with the hills of Malvern; which, here barren, and there cultivated, here all chalk, and there all verdure, reminded me of Box-hill, and gave me an immediate sensation of reflected as well as of visual pleasure, from giving to my new habitation some resemblance of Norbury Park.' However, the lodge proved too small, Burney recalling how the queen 'said she would show me her room. "*This*, ma'am!" cried I, as I entered it – "is *this* little room for your Majesty?" "O stay," cried she, laughing, "till you see your own before you call it little!"' Today, Sidney Lodge is located on the site of Fauconberg Lodge. Now used as a boarding house for the Ladies' College, a green plaque between two of the ground-floor windows records its illustrious past.

🐾 **Retrace your steps down Overton Road and along the continuation of Parabola Road.**
On your left at Royston, 9 Queen's Parade, you'll see a blue plaque commemorating the house (5) where Henry Skillicorne's great-grandson William Nash Skillicorne (1807–87) lived, later becoming Cheltenham's first mayor.
🐾 **Continue to the end of the road as it bends towards the right.**
Here, in the middle of the road where the Gordon Lamp (6) now stands, is the site of the Sherborne Well, not to be confused with the Sherborne Spa (see below). It was opened in 1803 but soon ran dry within a few years.

🐾 **Turn left down Montpellier Walk.** Here on the left-hand side you'll see the Rotunda building **(7)**, which is owned by Lloyds Bank.

★ **Montpellier Spa**

It was here that the Montpellier Spa was developed by Henry Thompson in 1809. Initially it consisted of a simple *cottage ornée* with wooden pillars, but was later replaced with a more elaborate stone building that could be used for balls and assemblies. In 1825 Henry's son, Pearson Thompson, commissioned the celebrated London architect J. B. Papworth to add a dome to the building, and henceforth it became known as the Rotunda. Measuring 50 feet in diameter, the interior of the dome was partially inspired by the Pantheon in Rome. Today, the neoclassical building belongs to Lloyds Bank, and you can still appreciate the concentric pale-blue panels, or *lacunaria*, of the dome's interior during the bank's opening

Gordon Lamp, site of the Sherborne Well.

hours. There is also the motto carved above the entrance: '*Infirmo capiti fluit utilis utilis alvo*' ('Our waters cure head and stomach aches').

Among the visitors to Thompson's spa was Elizabeth Barrett Browning, who penned the following verse in 1819: 'To taste those lucid streams, for e'en the walk / To Thompsons wells, a pleasant place to talk. / Then what bright crowds are seen – when there, / The young, the old, the plain, the fair – / "Neath Esculapius" fostering wings / All sipping the benignant springs / And music aids, with her melodious note / To force the sweet solutions down the throat.'

🐾 **Continue down Montpellier Walk until the top of The Promenade is reached.** Then turn right to face the impressive Queen's Hotel (**8**), site of the Sherborne Spa.

★ **Sherborne or Imperial Spa**

The Sherborne Spa, which later became known as the Imperial Spa, stood on the site of the Queen's Hotel. Modelled on Rome's Temple of Jupiter and embellished with a statue of Hygeia, the goddess of health, it proved so popular that the now famous Promenade, previously a scarcely passable marshy track, was built to connect it to the High Street. In fact, the tree-lined grandeur of The Promenade is still best appreciated from the upper storey windows of the Queen's. However, by 1837 a fall in the water table caused the well to run dry, and so the building was resited close to the Neptune Fountain, where it survived until 1937, when it was demolished and replaced by a cinema and then subsequently, in the 1980s, the Royscot House office building.

🦶 **Continue to the end of Imperial Square, passing the exquisite Imperial Fountain (see walk 9) on your right.**
🦶 **Turn right into Trafalgar Street, then immediately left into Montpellier Spa Road, and left again into Vittoria Walk.**
Towards the bottom on the right-hand side you'll find Vittoria House **(9)** which today is used as offices.

★ Hygeia House

Vittoria House, previously known as Hygeia House, was the residence of the Liverpool and London banker Henry Thompson when he lived here in 1804. It was here, prior to the success of his Montpellier Spa in 1809, that Thompson was able to dispense medicinal water after piping it through various boreholes sunk nearby.

🦶 **Cross Oriel Road and turn right until you reach the corner with Bath Road.**
Here you'll arrive at The Playhouse Theatre **(10)**, formerly home to Montpellier Baths. If the theatre is open it's well worth going inside to appreciate its interior, including some fine stained-glass windows.

Vittoria House, formerly Hygeia House.

★ Montpellier Baths

The Montpellier Baths, which were originally built in 1806, were initially used by Henry Thompson as a salts manufactory. The salt was distilled from the mineral water and sold in bottles. This allowed customers to benefit from the health-giving properties without having to visit the town. Nevertheless, success was fairly short-lived, and so Thompson also promoted bathing as an alternative to drinking the waters, mindful that the town was now beginning to suffer from increasing shortages of mineral water. In later years, the baths became a swimming pool, and subsequently the home of the Playhouse Theatre, the auditorium being built above the pool, with the stage positioned directly above the deep end.

🦶 **Retrace your steps and continue along Oriel Road.**
When you reach the corner with Rodney Road on your right, you'll see Rodney Road car park **(11)**.

★ Cambray Spa

Sadly, when the Rodney Road car park was built it demolished a small, octagonal Gothic-style building, which once housed the second site of the Cambray Spa. If desired, a short detour can now be taken to visit the site of the first Cambray Spa **(12)**. Located in a cottage known as Fowler's Cottage, this spa once stood in the angle formed by the footpath linking Cambray Place with Rodney Road. This chalybeate spa opened in 1807 but was later moved to the second site, where, combined with an additional well, it had the advantage of being able to offer both saline- and iron-impregnated waters. The spa operated from 1834 to 1873 until it was converted into a Turkish bath, where patrons could enjoy massage and a range of 'vapour, mercurial, sulphur, salt, alkaline, warm or cold, galvanic or electro chemical baths'. The building was demolished in 1938.

🦶 **Retrace your steps back to Oriel Road and turn right. Cross over Imperial Square to the left and enter the Town Hall (13).**

★ Central Spa

The Town Hall is the site of the Central Spa, which was opened in 1906 as part of the corporation's attempt to revive the spa. To the left of the entrance hall you'll find the octagonal counter with four elaborate marbled urns, only one of which now has a tap for dispensing the water. In its heyday it dispensed different types of water, both from Montpellier and Pittville.

🦶 **Turn right along the Promenade to walk to the Pittville Park Pump Room or to return to the starting point of the walk.**
No tour of Cheltenham's spas is complete without also visiting the magnificent Pump Room in Pittville Park **(16)**.
🦶 **At Boots Corner turn left to return along the path to Cheltenham Minster, or continue on to Pittville Park by turning right along the High Street and then left along Winchcombe Street, and then along Pittville Lawn, where you reach the entrance to the park with its recently restored gates.**
Alternatively, it is a short drive to Pittville Park, where there is ample parking adjacent to the Pump Room.

Above: The octagonal counter from the Central Spa in the Town Hall.

Left: Detail from window inside the Playhouse Theatre, formerly Montpellier Baths.

★ Columbia Place

One of the advantages of walking is the opportunity to appreciate the very fine architecture which exists in this part of the town. A good example is the attractive row of houses in Columbia Place, originally spelt Colombia Place (**14**), which today forms part of Winchcombe Street. Nevertheless, back in 1830 this wasn't a view appreciated by everyone. The politician, journalist and farmer William Cobbett (1763–1835), for example, wrote in *Rural Rides*, 'There is a new row of most gaudy and fantastical dwelling places called "Colombia Place", given it, doubtless, by some dealer in *bonds*.' Cobbett's view was part of his scathing attack on Cheltenham and was largely borne from his opposition to the leisure classes and support for impoverished farm labourers. To him Cheltenham was 'a nasty, ill-looking place, half clown and half cockney', and a place 'they call a "watering place"; that is to say, a place to which East India plunderers, West India floggers, English tax-gorgers, together with

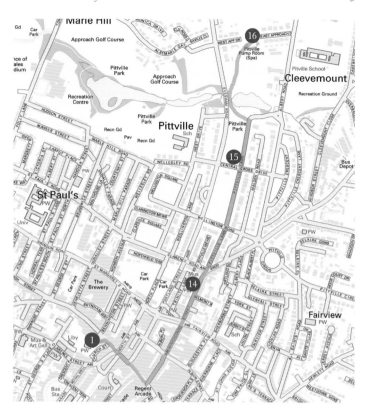

1. Cheltenham Minster
14. Colombia Place
15. Outdoor café
16. Pittville Pump Room

gluttons, drunkards, and debauchees of all descriptions, female as well as male, resort, at the suggestion of silently laughing quacks, in the hope of getting rid of the bodily consequences of their manifold sins and iniquities.' While Cobbett considered himself fully justified in his views, he was wrong about the 'dealer in *bonds*': in fact, Colombia Place was so called due to its construction being commissioned by a cavalry equipment supplier whose business interests extended to a salt-refining business in Colombia.

★ Little Spa

Another advantage of walking is the possibility of visiting the site of a subsidiary Pittville spa that predated even the opening of Pittville Pump Room. This site is located in the outdoor café (**15**) in Central Cross Drive. It still retains many original features, including the beautiful old spa tap. The spa, which became known as the Little Spa, opened in the 1820s and was housed in Essex Lodge. Being located on the town-centre side of the park, this spa was ideally accessible for those walking from the centre, and was probably initially only envisaged as a temporary arrangement during the construction of the main pump room. The lodge was demolished around 1903 and replaced by the present-day café.

★ Pittville Pump Room

Pittville Pump Room was designed as Cheltenham's most spectacular and prestigious spa. In fact, it has also been considered England's finest spa building. Commissioned in 1825 by lawyer and wealthy landowner Joseph Pitt as the focal point for his new town of Pittville, it took five

Pittville Pump Room.

years to build at a cost of £90,000. Its impressive Ionic columns were based on the Erechtheion originals in Athens, and the parapet figures of Hippocrates, 'father' of medicine, Hygeia, goddess of health, and Aesculapius, god of medicine and healing, although only copies of the originals, still add to its overall sense of grandeur. Unfortunately, however magnificent it was, it could do nothing to halt the decline in fashion for water drinking that was occurring during the 1830s, and so by the time the Scottish novelist Catherine Sinclair wrote about Pittville in 1838 she'd already witnessed the shattering of Pitt's dream of his new town: 'On Tuesday morning,' she wrote in *Hill and Valley*, 'we drove in a horse fly to visit Pitville [*sic*] in the suburbs of Cheltenham, a scene of gorgeous magnificence. Here a large estate has been divided into public gardens, and sprinkled with houses of every size, shape, and character; - Grecian temples, Italian villas, and citizen's boxes, so fresh and clean, you would imagine they were all blown out at once like soap-bubbles. A wealthy Mr. Pitt, who possessed a million of money, and did not think himself rich enough, built all those beautiful residences as a speculation; but the scheme failed, and he might have said, like Francis I, "all was lost but his honour."'

Despite being Pitt's loss it certainly became Cheltenham's gain, not only to have such an undeveloped area relatively close to the centre which eventually was transformed into its most famous public park, but also to be able to utilise the Pump Room as a venue for hosting concerts and a range of public and private events. Today, although the Pump Room doesn't currently dispense the water from its 80-foot-deep well, restoration of its pump/fountain, which is set in its galleried hall, took place as recently as the 1970s, and so the vestiges of its spa heritage are still visible.

👣 **Return to the town centre via the same route and then back to Cheltenham Minster (St Mary's).**

Walk 3

From Elysium to Hell

Distance: 2.5 miles

Minimum Time: 2 hours

Parking: Cheltenham Walk (located near Jessop Avenue), or Chester Walk.

Where to Eat and Drink: At start/end of walk The Cheltenham Dandy and Well Walk Tea Room, both in Well Walk, serve lunches, or visit The Wilson Café at the Museum & Gallery in Clarence Street. At the Beehive (1–3 Montpellier Villas) you can eat and drink in a pub that was once much frequented by the poet C. Day-Lewis. At The Strand (42 High Street) you can eat and drink at the house where Lord Byron and H. T. H. Bayly once lived.

Where to stay: Hanover House Bed and Breakfast at 65 St George's Road (Tel. 01242 541297, www.hanoverhouse.org) has several literary associations. Its Tennyson bedroom is named after Alfred Lord Tennyson, Poet Laureate, who was a resident of St James' Square, located to the rear of Hanover House. Its Rossetti bedroom is named after Christina Rossetti who provided poems for Sir Edward Elgar to put to music, and Elgar's wife, Alice, who was a writer and poet, lived here from 1859 to 1861. At The Bradley (19 Bayshill Road, tel. 01242 519077) you can stay in a hotel which was home to the preacher Revd Charles Bradley whose son, A. C. Bradley, became the foremost Shakespearean scholar of his time.

Cheltenham Public Library with the statue of Shakespeare on its pediment.

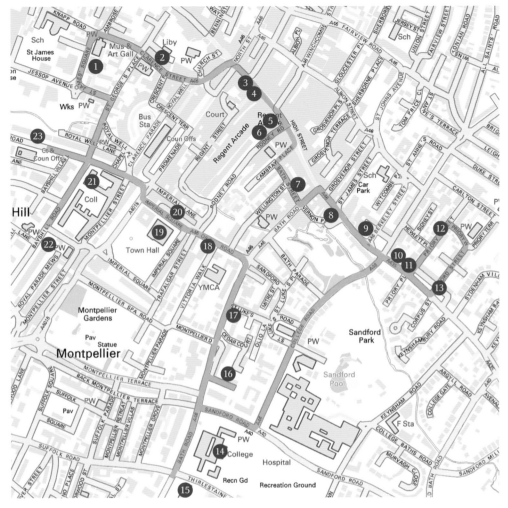

1. 10 St James' Square
2. Public Library
3. 148 High Street
4. Entrance to Regent's Arcade
5. Site of the Assembly Rooms
6. Rodney Lodge
7. 16 Bath Street
8. 42 High Street
9. Cedar House

10. 2–6 London Road
11. Site of the Priory
12. 28 Priory Street
13. Priory Parade
14. Cheltenham College
15. Thirlestaine House
16. 5 Paragon Terrace
17. 96 Bath Road
18. 3 Wolseley Terrace

19. Town Hall
20. 6 Imperial Square
21. Cheltenham Ladies' College
22. 19 Bayshill Road
23. Hanover House

The actor and playwright David Garrick once said on leaving Cheltenham to return to London that it was like 'leaving Elysium to arrive at Hell'. Heaven or Hell? Both have been used to describe Cheltenham. A character from E. M. Forster's *Howard's End* (1910) states categorically that she'd 'live anywhere except Bournemouth, Torquay, and Cheltenham'. William Cobbett in his *Rural Rides* (1830) called the town 'a nasty, ill-looking place, half clown and half cockney' and a 'resort of the lame and the lazy, the gormandizing and guzzling.' Thirteen years later Thomas Carlyle was equally unimpressed, writing to his wife, 'We saw only the roofs and steeples of Cheltenham; quite enough for me.' Whereas when Matthew Arnold wrote to his mother he mused, 'I should like very well to be going to Cheltenham now ... to stay a fortnight in that very cheerful place for ... Cheltenham itself and the country about it is as pleasant as anything in England.' Love it or hate it, writers have always flocked here ever since it was a fashionable place and, even more so, since the birth of its literature festival in 1949. This walk celebrates the town's numerous literary connections, from poet laureates to 'vello-maniacs', from the National Poet of Australia to the discovery of 'Jeeves'.

For an extended literary walk, this walk may be combined with walk 5, 'Through the Looking Glass', by connecting from site 13 on this walk to site 6 on the Charlton Kings one. Allow twenty minutes one-way to do this, by walking up London Road and turning right into Cudnall Street.

The walk may be extended still further by visiting Cheltenham cemetery at Bouncers Lane, where there are several graves of interest. These include the poet and dramatist James Elroy Flecker, whose grave is located in section W/20306, and who wrote the poem 'November Eves', which starts 'November Evenings! Damp and still / They used to cloak Leckhampton hill'. Also the poet Charles Turner, brother of Alfred Lord Tennyson, who is buried in grave X 4826, and the writer and poet W. H. Davies, whose ashes are scattered in Garden 1. Davies became famous for spending his life as a tramp, and gave an account in his *Autobiography of a Super-Tramp* (1907) of how he was arrested by the police on two separate occasions in a case of mistaken identity 'for that affair in Cheltenham'. Enquiries may be made at the cemetery and crematorium office (open Monday to Friday 9 a.m. – 5 p.m.; 9.30 a.m. opening on Wednesday) to help with the location of the graves.

 The walk starts at 10 St James' Square (1).

★ **Alfred Lord Tennyson**

It was in this house, once described as a 'tall, old-fashioned villa, built in the most approved doll's house style of architecture', where the poet **Alfred Lord Tennyson** (1809–92) lived from 1846 to 1850. Following his father's death, Tennyson had invested his family's inheritance and the earnings from his poetry in woodcarving machinery. However, the venture failed, causing his twin demons of melancholia and hypochondria to surface again. Tennyson's personal happiness was therefore threatened when he moved to Cheltenham to stay with his mother and sisters who were renting the house. Nevertheless, it appears to have been a most productive time for the poet. He worked in a little attic room in the house, 'not kept in very orderly fashion', with books and papers strewn 'as much on the floor and the chairs as upon the table'. Visiting friends remembered him reading passages from Shakespeare's *Pericles* and *Love's Labour's Lost*, but also 'pipe in mouth, discours[ing] ... more unconstrainedly than anywhere else on men and things and what death means'. Still mourning the death of his beloved Cambridge friend Arthur Hallam, Tennyson also wrote part of *In Memoriam* (1849) here, the stanzas commencing 'Calm and deep peace on this high wold' said to be a description of the Cotswolds. Tennyson also displayed his family's love of animals when he 'bribed one of the officials [at Cheltenham's St James' Station, located behind the house] for the temporary possession of a highly educated parrot, which was a pet of the railway men, and was wont to impart unauthorised information to the passengers'. His mother, who was a 'rather unconventional old lady, seldom went out of doors unless accompanied by two at least of the three or four dogs which – not to mention a monkey – belonged to the establishment'.

The house where Tennyson lived from 1846 to 1850.

👣 Turn right into Clarence Street and arrive at the public library (2) on your left.

★ Cheltenham Public Library
Built in 1887–9, the public library also once accommodated the Schools of Art and Science on its first floor. Notice on the pediment the statue of Shakespeare which, unfortunately, lost its pen during previous refurbishment work.

👣 Stop here if you wish for a drink at The Cheltenham Dandy, Well Walk Tea Room or The Wilson Café.
👣 Continue along Clarence Street and turn right at Boots Corner into the High Street.

For a long time the only street in the town, the High Street, which in earlier times was also known as The Great Street or Cheltenham Street, has often featured in literary works. Johanna Schopenhauer, the mother of the German philosopher, for example, wrote in her *Travels in England and Scotland* (1803) that 'Cheltenham consists of a single street, at least one mile long, from which small side streets radiate with single buildings. On this main street there are elegant buildings, glittering shops, lending libraries and cafés.'

👣 Proceed to 148 High Street (3) on your right.

★ Lillah McCarthy
It was on this site, now occupied by Burger King, that the actress Lillah McCarthy (1875–1960) was born. She became one of the leading actresses of her day. In her autobiography she described Cheltenham as 'a perfect setting for a life of well-bred retirement, a place where people grown old in the service of their country find peace and modest comfort'.

👣 Proceed three doors down to the entrance of the Regent Arcade (4) on your right.

★ The Plough
Just inside the entrance on the left is a green plaque, which records this as the former site of The Plough, Cheltenham's leading hotel and coaching inn, which dates back to 1654. It was from here that fast stagecoaches such as the Cheltenham Flyer set out to London, arriving there within ten and a half hours by 1826. Sadly, the hotel was demolished in 1980. Its yard, now occupied by the shopping centre, was reputed to be the largest in the country; it could accommodate 100 horses and included a number of coach houses. In its heyday the hotel provided lodgings for several famous writers, even if it did not always meet their expectations; the American essayist Washington Irving, for example, stayed here on 1 August 1815, but the assessment he jotted down in his journal was 'not very good'. Despite this, the hotel was always viewed as the place 'to be seen': the journalist C. M. Westmacott, writing under the pseudonym

of Bernard Blackmantle in *English Spy* (1826), commented that 'if you wish to make a figure among the Chelts and be thought any thing of, you will, of course, domicile at the Plough'.

🦶 **Continue to Lloyds bank (5) on your right, located on the corner of Rodney Road.**

★ Assembly Rooms

This is the former site of the Assembly Rooms. It was here that Charles Dickens (1812–70), William Makepeace Thackeray (1811–63) and Oscar Wilde (1854–1900) gave public performances. Dickens first visited the town in October 1859, but made more frequent visits during the 1860s so that he could visit his friend, the actor William Charles Macready (see walk 8), who came to retire at 6 Wellington Square. 'It happened that I read at Cheltenham a couple of months ago,' Dickens once wrote to Macready, adding 'I have rarely seen a place that so attracted my fancy.' This was also the place where Charles Dodgson (1832–98), better known as Lewis Carroll, is reputed to have found his inspiration for the Cheshire Cat. Accompanied by Alice and her sisters, Carroll went to see the illusionist Herr Döbler perform a show on 6 April 1863. One of the illusions Döbler conducted was Professor Pepper's 'celebrated ghost illusion', in which plate glass and lighting was used to give the impression of objects appearing or disappearing. Following this visit, Carroll added the 'Pig and Pepper' chapter to *Alice's Adventures in Wonderland* (1865), and included the celebrated description of the Cheshire Cat which 'vanished quite slowly, beginning with the end of the tail, and ending with the grin, which remained some time after the rest of it had gone'.

🦶 **Turn right into Rodney Road and proceed to Rodney Lodge (6) on your right.**

Rodney Lodge, now used by Inlingua as a language school, was originally built with its attractive Ionic porch columns in 1809 by Robert Hughes, the son of the owner of the Assembly Rooms.

★ James Payn

It was also the birthplace of the novelist and editor James Payn (1830–98). A friend of Charles Dickens and Wilkie Collins, his forty-six novels achieved only minor success. His collections of short stories showed a fertile imagination, even predicting technological advances such as air conditioning and the Channel Tunnel. However, he is perhaps best known for his verse on buttered toast: 'I had never had a piece of toast / Particularly long and wide, / But fell upon the sanded floor, / And always on the buttered side.'

🦶 **Return to the High Street and turn right. Turn right again into Cambray Place.**

Notice at No. 30 Jessop House, currently occupied by Bistrot Coco, a bronze plaque which records this as the birthplace of the cricketer Gilbert Jessop (1874–1955), who became a childhood hero for the actress Lillah McCarthy.

🦶 **Turn left and proceed to 16 Bath Street (7) on your left.**

★ The Garrick's Head

This is the building of the former pub The Garrick's Head, which was sold in 1998 and is now awaiting redevelopment. It still retains a plasterwork model of the head of the actor David Garrick

(1717–79) on its façade. Previously this was the site of the Theatre Royal, a major entertainment venue for the town from 1805, when it opened, until 1839, when it was destroyed by fire.

🦶 **Turn left into Bath Road. Then turn right and proceed to 42 High Street (8) where, at The Strand, you can also stop to eat and drink.**

★ **Lord Byron and N. T. H. Bayly**
It was here at 430 (now 42) High Street that Lord Byron first lodged when he visited Cheltenham, describing it as 'the sordid inn'. It was also here that the poet and playwright Nathaniel Thomas Haynes Bayly (1797–1839) once lived (see also walk 4). Shortly after his marriage to Helena Beecher Hayes, which took place in Cheltenham on 11 July 1826, Bayly composed one of his best-known ballads, 'I'd Be a Butterfly Born in a Bower.'

🦶 **Proceed to Cedar House (9) on your left, just before the junction with Berkeley Street.**

★ **Belle Vue Hotel**
Cedar House now comprises residential flats. Originally known as Belle Vue, it was built as a private house before 1800, and later became a hotel. It was here that the Cheltenham and Gloucester Building Society began in 1850, and in April 1863, when it was known as Belle Vue Hotel, Lewis Carroll stayed here for four days while visiting the Liddell family at Hetton Lawn, Charlton Kings (see walk 5).

🦶 **Proceed past the junction with Hewlett Road to 2–6 London Road (10) on your left.**

★ **Sir Walter Scott**
This terrace of four houses was formerly known as Oxford Buildings. In fact, the name is still visible, having been carved into the stonework. It was here that Sir Walter Scott stayed for two days in November 1826 with his sister-in-law while taking the waters. However, it's unlikely that he enjoyed the experience, having written earlier, 'I have had as many remedies sent me for cramp and jaundice as would set up a quack doctor ... besides all sort of recommendations to go to Cheltenham, to Harrowgate, to Jericho for aught I know. Now if there is one thing I detest more than another, it is a watering-place.'

🦶 **Continue to the junction with Priory Street (11) on your left.**

★ **Josephine Butler**
This was the site of The Priory, a fine Regency house, where the social reformer Josephine Butler (1828–1906) lived from 1857 to 1866, following her husband's appointment as vice principal at Cheltenham College. The present-day Wellington Mansions building, built in 1999, replaced The Priory, which was demolished in 1968, echoing the architecture of the original building and incorporating a commemorative blue plaque on its façade. It was here in 1864 that the Butlers suffered a terrible personal tragedy. One evening, their six-year-old daughter Eva fell from the banisters when she was running to greet her parents and died in her father's arms. Josephine blamed herself because she had previously rebuked Eva for being late for tea. Eva was later buried at St Peter's church in Leckhampton. This tragic experience was a turning

point in Josephine's life and, following the Butlers' move to Liverpool in 1864, she 'became possessed with an irresistible urge to go forth and find some pain keener than my own, to meet with people more unhappy than myself'. In Liverpool she began her groundbreaking work campaigning for women's rights, in particular campaigning against their degrading treatment under the Contagious Diseases Act. In later years when she returned to Cheltenham she even uncovered unsavoury facts about high-class prostitution in the town and the use of *maisons tolérées*. Aside from this unpleasantness, she was gladdened by a 'curious & comforting feeling of companionship in being so near Eva's grave'.

🦶 Turn left and proceed to 28 Priory Street (12).

★ Adam Lindsay Gordon
This Regency town house, called Court House, is where the poet Adam Lindsay Gordon (1833–70) lived. Gordon attended school at Cheltenham College, where his father was the Hindustani master. Gordon had a somewhat raffish adolescence, spending much of the time bare-knuckle boxing and steeplechasing. He witnessed Cheltenham's first steeplechase, held at Noverton Lane in 1847, when one of the horses was killed and the rider narrowly escaped death. This experience made a deep impression on Gordon, who was only thirteen at the time, and the experience later inspired him to write *How We Beat the Favourite* (1869), in which he imagined himself riding the mythical horse 'Bay Iseult' to win against 'The Clown' by 'a short head'. Although he used poetic licence in this poem, Gordon himself was an accomplished rider, and rode in the Berkeley Hunt Cup Steeplechase at Prestbury in 1852. A year later he emigrated to Australia, where he became the National Poet of Australia as well as a champion jockey. Court House is referenced in his poem 'An Exile's Farewell' (1853), in which he writes, 'How vivid Recollection's hand / Recalls the scene once more! / I see the same tall poplars stand / Beside the garden door; / I see the bird-cage hanging still; / And where my sister set / The flowers in the window-sill — / Can they be living yet?'

🦶 Turn right into Priory Walk (immediately opposite Court House) and then right into Oxford Street.
Once known as Pritchard's Passage, Priory Walk was ironically described in 1839 as 'a locality of no mean notoriety of everything modest, genteel, pure and virtuous that is to be found in Cheltenham', following a failed attempt by Thomas Pritchard, one of the residents, to bring a charge of keeping a disorderly house against one of the families in the neighbourhood.
🦶 Continue towards the end of the street and look back at the terrace of Priory Parade (13).

★ Jane Austen
This fine terrace was previously known as Oxford Parade, and it has been used as a location for several film and television adaptations of nineteenth-century novels, including the 1995 version of Jane Austen's *Pride and Prejudice* which starred Colin Firth, Jennifer Ehle and Julia Sawalha. Jane Austen visited Cheltenham for three weeks in 1816 and was aggrieved to hear that her sister was charged three guineas a week for her lodging and accused the landlady of charging for 'the *name* of the High Street'. Although she found the Cheltenham waters agreeable, she commented to her sister that 'everything else [in Cheltenham] is trifling'.

The terraced houses formerly known as Oxford Parade, one of the locations used for the 1995 version of Jane Austen's *Pride and Prejudice*.

👣 **Cross London Road and turn right. Then take second left into College Road.**
Originally known as Sir Matthew Wood's Road after a banking family who owned land in the Sandford area, it subsequently became known as College Road by the late 1860s, following the founding of Cheltenham College in 1841.

👣 **Turn right into Sandford Road and then left into Bath Road to see Cheltenham College (14) on your left.**

★ **Jeeves**
The college has a plethora of literary associations, including the fact that Irish-born poet laureate C. Day-Lewis once taught at the junior school. It has also helped to educate many future writers, including the English-born Australian novelist Patrick White (1912–90), who won the Nobel Prize in Literature in 1973. Also, it was here at the college cricket ground that P. G. Wodehouse (1881–1975) discovered his 'Jeeves'. Recalling the time when he had watched Warwickshire play Gloucestershire he wrote, 'I suppose Jeeves' bowling must have impressed me, for I remembered him in 1916, when I was in New York and just starting the Jeeves and Bertie saga, and it was just the name I wanted.' Sadly, Percy Jeeves, the Warwickshire bowler whom Wodehouse admired so greatly, was killed in action in July 1916 during the First World War.

👣 **You can stop here to eat or drink by walking along the back of Montpellier Terrace to visit The Beehive at 1–3 Montpellier Villas, which was once a favourite haunt of C. Day-Lewis.**

👣 **Continue on, crossing the next junction, to see Thirlestaine House (15) on your left.**

★ Sir Thomas Phillipps

This was where the collector of books and manuscripts Sir Thomas Phillipps (1792–1872) once lived. Phillipps was an obsessive bibliophile who, at one stage, aimed to acquire a copy of every book in the world. He even coined the term 'vello-maniac' to describe his life's obsession. When he bought Thirlestaine House in 1867, it took two years and 250 men to transport his library across the Cotswolds in a wagon train. Following the move, Phillipps noted that his wife complained that she was 'booked out of one wing and ratted out of the other'. Notice the replica Parthenon sculptures which adorn the building.

🐾 Turn around, proceed down Bath Road and take the third right to 5 Paragon Terrace (16).

One of the sculptures from the façade of Thirlestaine House, once home to Sir Thomas Phillipps' vast collection of books and manuscripts.

★ Anthony Trollope

This was the house where Anthony Trollope stayed when he visited Cheltenham from December 1852 until April 1853. At that time he was a Post Office surveyor who was attempting to introduce postal deliveries on a Sunday. However, his attempts were strongly opposed by the preacher Revd Francis Close (see walk 4), whose reputation as the town's 'Pope' was well known. Although Close won the day in the end, Trollope never forgot his bitter battle fought against Close and later, in his novel *Miss Mackenzie* (1865), portrayed him as Mr Stumfold, who 'was always fighting the devil by opposing those pursuits which are the life and mainstay of such places as Littlebath', 'Littlebath' being the name that Trollope used to portray Cheltenham. Inevitably, the novel included the 'Stumfoldian edict ... ordaining that no Stumfoldian in Littlebath should be allowed to receive a letter on Sundays'.

🐾 Return to Bath Road and turn right. Proceed to Belmore House, 96 Bath Road (17) on your right.

★ C. Day-Lewis

This was the house that C. Day-Lewis rented when he first moved to Cheltenham. Later, he borrowed £600 to buy the freehold for Box Cottage in Charlton Kings (see walk 5).

🐾 Continue down Bath Road. Turn left into Oriel Road. Just after the junction with Vittoria Walk turn left to see 3 Wolseley Terrace (18) on your right.

★ P. G. Wodehouse

This house, which at the time of writing is known as Isbourne House, was the house where P. G. Wodehouse's parents lived. Wodehouse, who loved cricket, stayed at the house on 13 August 1913 and the next day walked from here to the Cheltenham College ground to see Warwickshire play Gloucestershire, where he was to discover his 'Jeeves'. Another incident connected with Wodehouse and Cheltenham occurred in December 2013 when the *Gloucestershire Echo* tested the honesty of the local people by putting into practice Wodehouse's habit of, rather than posting his stamped and addressed letters himself, relying on the public-spirited nature of the general public to find and pick them up when he threw them from his fourth-floor window, and deposit them in a pillar box. The *Echo*'s experiment resulted in fifteen out of the eighteen letters left in public places being dutifully posted, and a spokesman for the P. G. Wodehouse Society commented that Wodehouse 'would have been delighted to know that the people of Cheltenham were as trustworthy now as he found them then'.

🐾 Return to Oriel Road. Turn left, continuing into Imperial Square, to see the Town Hall (19) on your left.

★ William Makepeace Thackeray

The Town Hall has been used as a location for several film adaptations of nineteenth-century novels, including the 1998 version of *Vanity Fair* by William Makepeace Thackeray (1847–48), which starred Philip Glenister, Nathaniel Parker, and Natasha Little. Thackeray described Cheltenham as a place 'wherever trumps and frumps were found together; wherever scandal was cackled'. There is a memorable scene in the novel in which Jos Sedley drives in an open carriage and wishes that 'all Cheltenham, all Chowringhee, all Calcutta' could see him in all of his finery, with his attractive companions.

🐾 Cross over to 6 Imperial Square (20), which is directly opposite the Town Hall.

★ Charles Turner

This is the house, currently occupied by a printer's shop, where the poet Charles Turner (formerly Tennyson, 1808–79) died at the age of seventy. Charles was Alfred Tennyson's favourite brother and their shared interest in poetry was revealed at an early age through their collaboration on *Poems by Two Brothers* (1829). While Alfred explored a variety of poetic forms, Charles concentrated almost exclusively on writing sonnets. After the death of his great uncle, Charles changed his name to Turner, in deference to the terms of his uncle's will, although he also became known under the sobriquet 'Tennyson Turner'. When Turner died, fifty unpublished sonnets were discovered in the house and were later added to his *Collected Poems* (1880). He was buried in the town cemetery in Bouncers Lane, Prestbury, where a stone cross marks his grave. Before leaving here, notice the attractive 'double heart' pattern of the fine ironwork along this terrace.

🐾 Continue to the end of Imperial Square, cross over and turn right into St George's Road to see Cheltenham Ladies' College (21) on your left.

★ **Cheltenham Ladies' College**

The college has many literary associations, including the fact that the poet U. A. Fanthorpe (1929–2009) taught English here for sixteen years. Many well-known writers received part of their education at the college, including D. K. Broster (1877–1950), May Sinclair (1863–1946), and Margaret Kennedy (1896–1967). The college also contains a hall called the Princess Hall, which was named after Tennyson's poem of the same name, which advocates women's rights.

🐾 **Turn left and proceed to 19 Bayshill Road (22).**

Here you'll find The Bradley Hotel, which was the retirement home of the preacher Revd Charles Bradley, whose son, A. C. Bradley (1851–1935), became the most celebrated Shakespearean scholar, as demonstrated by the following anonymous poem: 'I dreamt last night that Shakespeare's Ghost / Sat for a civil service post. / The English paper for that year / Had several questions on King Lear / Which Shakespeare answered very badly / Because he hadn't read his Bradley.'

🐾 **Return to St George's Road, turning right and crossing over to No. 65 (23).**

★ **Hanover House**

This house, formerly 4 York Terrace, is where the writer, poet and inspiration to Sir Edward Elgar, Lady Caroline Alice Elgar, *née* Roberts (1848–1920), lived from 1859 to 1861. It is likely that Alice occupied the uppermost room in the house, which may have doubled up as her schoolroom, since while her brothers attended Cheltenham College as day pupils, Alice received her private education at home. In 1888, when she announced her intention to marry Elgar, her family was so horrified at the thought of her marrying a relatively poor musician (who was also a Roman Catholic) that they disinherited her from the family fortune. Alice wrote many poems, which Elgar set to music, and in 1898 he dedicated the first of the *Enigma Variations* (1899) to her. Another historic resident of Hanover House was Colonel John Shakespear who, as a captain at 'The Charge of the Light Brigade', may have known Alfred Lord Tennyson. When the Light Brigade was ordered to advance along 'the valley of Death', Shakespear and his troop attempted to provide essential artillery support. However, the manoeuvre failed because of the difficult local terrain. Afterwards, as a personal witness to the terrible massacre, Shakespear wrote letters to *The Times* outlining his views at a time when controversy raged about the action taken. It seems likely that when Tennyson, in December 1854, still resident in Cheltenham, came to write his classic poem, drawing on the account published in *The Times*, he may have heard a first-hand account from his near neighbour, John Shakespear, who lived just 300 metres away.

🐾 **Turn around and then turn left into St George's Place. Take the third left into St James' Square, turning right at the roundabout to return to Tennyson's house on your right.**

Walk 4
Spiritual Advantages

Distance: 4 miles

Minimum Time: 2 hours 45 mins

Parking: Chester Walk (nearest) or Cheltenham Walk (located near Jessop Avenue).

Where to Eat and Drink: At Zizzi's (Tel. 01242 252493, www.zizzi.co.uk/venue/index/ cheltenham) you can still appreciate the Gothic architecture of St James' church, from which the restaurant has been converted. At start/end of walk, The Cheltenham Dandy and Well Walk Tea Rooms, both in Well Walk, serve snacks and lunches, or visit The Wilson Café at the Art Gallery & Museum in Clarence Street. Gianni Ristorante at 1 Royal Well Place may also be visited during the walk.

Where to stay: At The Bradley (19 Bayshill Road, www.thebradleyhotel.co.uk, tel. 01242 519077) you can stay in a hotel that was home to the preacher Revd Charles Bradley, whose son, A. C. Bradley, became the foremost Shakespearean scholar.

Cheltenham College Chapel with its 'glorious soaring architecture'.

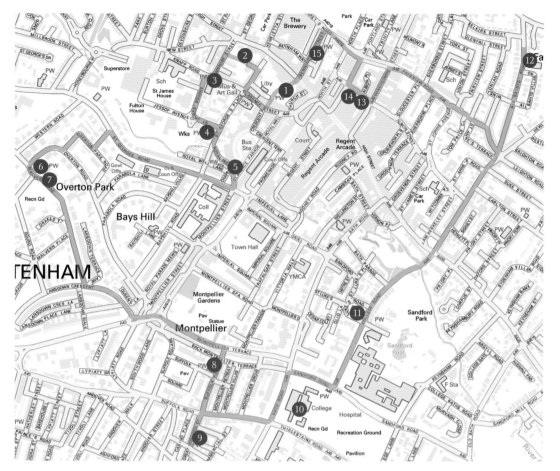

1. Cheltenham Minster
2. Cheltenham Chapel
3. St Gregory's church
4. The Synagogue
5. Bayshill Unitarian church

6. Christ church
7. The Grange
8. St James' church
9. Bethesda church
10. Cheltenham College Chapel

11. St Luke's church
12. All Saints' church
13. Site of the Corn Exchange
14. Site of the Mechanics Institute
15. Cheltenham Spiritualist church

'There are great spiritual advantages to be had in that town ...' So declares Bulstrode, one of the characters from George Eliot's *Middlemarch* (1872), about Cheltenham, a place which few towns can rival for its wealth of churches and chapels. Its reputation as a leading evangelical centre was principally developed by Francis Close (1797–1882) who, from 1826, became perpetual curate of Cheltenham parish church for the next thirty years. Dubbed 'the Pope of Cheltenham' by Alfred Tennyson, Close was a forceful and at times controversial preacher who came to dominate much of Cheltenham's life. It was Close's opposition to postal deliveries on Sundays, for example, that brought him into conflict with Anthony Trollope (see walk 3) who was then, as Post Office surveyor, attempting to introduce this service to the town. While Close's sabbatarian views prevailed at the time, Trollope never forgot his bitter battle against the preacher, and so later on, when he wrote his novel *Miss Mackenzie* (1865), Trollope satirised Close, portraying him as Mr Stumfold, who 'was always fighting the devil by opposing those pursuits which are the life and mainstay of such places as Littlebath', Littlebath being the name that Trollope gave to Cheltenham.

This walk celebrates many of the town's landmarks that have inspired different faiths and beliefs. It starts at the medieval parish church in the heart of the town, and takes in hidden gems, including its fine synagogue, as well as other well-known and less well-known sites. Where relevant, contact details have been provided to enable visits to be made by prior arrangement.

👣 **The walk starts at Cheltenham Minster (St Mary's) (1).**

★ **Cheltenham Minster (St Mary's)**

The church, which has recently been made Cheltenham Minster in recognition of its central role in the civic and religious life of the town, is open to visitors Monday–Friday 11 a.m. – 3 p.m. The church features several attractive stained-glass windows, most notably a superb circular rose window and one portraying the Last Supper. It also boasts several interesting memorials, including to Henry Skillicorne, the developer of the spa, and Hannah Forty, one of the spa pumpers (see walk 2), as well as 'the sad memoriall' of John English, a doctor in divinity who became the curate out of love for the cause of religion but was imprisoned by the Puritans for eighteen weeks, as a result of which, it is implied, his wife died from a broken heart. The most famous curate of St Mary's, however, was Francis Close, a keen evangelical who was also an influential figure in the development of Cheltenham as a centre for education and teacher training. In the churchyard, on the north-east side, are the remains of a fourteenth-century preaching cross from which John Wesley (1703–91) once preached. However, the townsfolk left a poor impression on him. During

Cheltenham Minster (St Mary's).

his visit on 8 May 1744 he recorded, 'I preached [at Cheltenham] on, "By grace are ye saved through faith," to a company who seemed to understand just as much of the matter, as if I had been talking Greek.' His final visit to Cheltenham in 1784 did not fare much better. On this occasion he recorded that 'I preached at noon to half a houseful of hearers, most of them cold and dead enough.' Before leaving the churchyard it's worth visiting the tombstone, located near the path on the east side of the church, commemorating John Higgs, who died in 1825. The amusing epitaph reads, 'Here lies John Higgs / for killing pigs was his delight / both morning, afternoon and night / both heats and colds he did endure / which no Physician could one cure, / his knife is laid, his work is done, / hope to heaven his soul is gone.' If you have sharp eyes you will also be able to find on the south side of the churchyard path brass measuring marks, approximately 7 centimetres in length, which were once used by traders to check the measurements of rope and cloth.

🦶 **Leave St Mary's churchyard via Well Walk and turn right into Clarence Street.**
You will pass St Matthew's church on your left. This was built in 1879 but its spire and tower were later removed for safety reasons.

🦶 **Turn right into St George's Place and then left into Jenner Walk.**
At the end of Jenner Walk you'll find Cheltenham Chapel's original building (**2**).

★ **Cheltenham Chapel**
Converted into offices today, Cheltenham Chapel was once an important focal point for the town's religious fervour. It was built in 1809, as the inscription on its stuccoed façade records, and is the town's earliest surviving Nonconformist chapel. One of its preachers, Rowland Hill (1744–1833), was a friend of Dr Edward Jenner (1749–1823), the pioneer of the smallpox vaccination, who lived at No. 8 (subsequently rebuilt and renumbered as 22) St George's Place between 1796 and 1820. As a result of their friendship, vaccination clinics were held in the chapel on Sundays following the religious service. In 1810 the chapel purchased the bottom end of Jenner's garden for use as a burial ground, and today the graveyard is a public open space known as Jenner Gardens. There are four interpretation boards within the gardens, telling the story of Jenner's life, the history of the chapel, the graveyard and the gardens. An interesting exploration may be made here of the surrounding memorial stones, which include 'Henry John … / who was unfortunately drowned / whilst bathing in the river Severn / … in the 17th year of his age', and John Ross, who has been commemorated with typically Victorian poetic effusion: 'Forgive blest shade the tributary tear / that mourns thy exit from a world like this. / Forgive the wish that would have kept thee here / and stayed thy progress to the realms of bliss. / No more confined to growing scenes of night / no more a tenent pent in mortal clay. / Now should we rather hail thy glorious flight / and trace thy journey to the realms of day.'

🦶 **Exit from behind Cheltenham Chapel via the lane that borders the left-hand side of the bowling green. At the end of this lane turn left into Ambrose Street. Turn right at the mini-roundabout and then left at the next one into St James' Square.**
Immediately on your left is the entrance to St Gregory's church (**3**).

★ **St Gregory's Church**
St Gregory's Roman Catholic church (www.stgregorys.org.uk, email: gregchurch.cheltenham @cliftondiocese.com) dates from 1854, but was built on the site of an earlier chapel of 1810, where members of the French royal family once worshipped. It was designed by the famous architect Charles Hansom (1817–88) of Clifton, in the Decorated Gothic style. Its magnificent 208-foot-high spire, which is 41 feet higher than the parish church, provides an indication of the town's early large Catholic population, which developed in particular during the Napoleonic Wars as French exiles fled the Continent to settle in Cheltenham.

🦶 **Continue to the roundabout, then turn left and immediately right into Synagogue Lane.**
On your left is the entrance to the synagogue (**4**).

★ Cheltenham Synagogue

The synagogue (www.cheltenhamsynagogue.org.uk, email: info@cheltenhamsynagogue.org.uk) is recognised as 'an outstanding example of a small provincial English synagogue'. Designed by William Hill Knight (*c.* 1812–94) – the same architect who later created the town's fashionable Montpellier Walk shopping precinct adorned with caryatids – it opened in 1839 to cater for the growing Jewish population following King George III's visit in 1788. Its Ashkenazi furniture, the oldest in the country, dates back to 1761, and some of its plaques are from as early as 1727. One of its principal attractions, however, is its dome, built by Nicholas Adams and described by the *Cheltenham Free Press* as being 'finished in a superior manner with cornice and fretwork'. Although the synagogue closed in 1903 due to a declining congregation, it reopened in 1939 following an influx of refugees and evacuees, and still maintains a flourishing membership today.

Continue to the end of Synagogue Lane and turn left. Cross over St George's Place and continue along Royal Well Place. Then turn left into Chapel Walk.
On your right, immediately next to Gianni Ristorante, where you can stop for food or drink, is the original building of the Bayshill Unitarian church (**5**), which is now occupied by the Cotswold Auction Company.

★ Bayshill Unitarian Church

It is interesting to note that the Unitarian church, which was built in 1844 in Anglo-Norman style, was the venue in 1936 for an important sermon preached by the Islamic scholar Abdullah Yusuf Ali (1872–1953) to a packed congregation. Best known for his translation of the Qur'an, which is one of the most widely used versions in the English language, Ali's support for

Interior of the synagogue's dome.

religious harmony between the East and West and his belief in the unity between all religions struck a deep chord with the congregation.

🦶 **Continue to the end of Chapel Walk and turn right into St George's Road.**
You'll pass the Ladies' College on your left.

🦶 **Turn left into Overton Park Road. Turn right at the T-junction and then, after the road bends round to the left, turn right and then left into Malvern Road.**
Christ church (**6**) is immediately on the left, directly opposite the mini-roundabout.

★ Christ Church

As Cheltenham's population increased tenfold between 1800 and 1840, several new churches were planned and built. One of these was Christ church (www.christchurchcheltenham.org.uk, tel. 01242 578163), which was developed through a project led by Francis Close. The architects were R. W. and C. Jearrad, who also designed the Queen's Hotel. The church was consecrated in 1840 but, unusually, this was before the surrounding houses were built. The church has many interesting features, including memorials associated with India and the Bengal civil service, as well as a noticeboard in the porch that harks back to the age of pre-motorised transport with its instructions that 'chairs are not allowed to take up at this door or stand in the any part of the carriageway.' Christ church's most famous preacher was Revd Frederick W. Robertson (1816–53) who served from 1842 to 1847. At one time he was considered to be the greatest preacher of the century, and it was said to be 'impossible to listen to this tall, auburn-haired young man without feeling emotion on account of that indescribable voice of his.'

Lansdown Crescent.

🦶 Continue 100 metres to The Grange (7) on your left.

★ The Grange

This villa, as indicated by the blue plaque on its wall, was where Francis Close, 'perpetual curate of Cheltenham', lived from 1839 to 1856. Originally built in 1838, the house provides evidence of Close's immense popularity since it was provided by subscriptions from his parishioners.

🦶 Continue to the end of Malvern Road and turn left into Lansdown Crescent.

Originally this large convex crescent, which dates back to the 1830s and was 'without equal in its day', was conceived by its architect, John B. Papworth, as comprising semi-detached villas, rather than a continuous terrace.

🦶 Turn left and then at the roundabout take the second exit into Montpellier Terrace.

🦶 Then turn right at the pelican crossing into Suffolk Parade.

At the corner with Suffolk Square you'll see St James' church (8), which has now been converted into Zizzi's restaurant.

🦶 There are several cafés, bars and restaurants located here, including The Daffodil (18–20 Suffolk Parade) and Moka Coffee House (14 Suffolk Parade).

★ St James' Church

The church, which was also known as Suffolk church, was built in 1825–30 and designed by the local architect Edward Jenkins in the Perpendicular style. Inside there used to be a memorial to the poet and playwright Nathaniel Thomas Haynes Bayly (1797–1839), which described him as 'a kind parent and affectionate husband, a popular author, and an accomplished gentleman'. Although he was famous for poems such as 'I'd Be a Butterfly' and 'She Wore a Wreath of Roses', his work was often the subject of ridicule.

🦶 Proceed to the end of Suffolk Parade and then continue into Great Norwood Street.

On the left, just before the junction with Chapel Lane, is Bethesda church (9).

★ Bethesda Church

This small chapel (www.bethesda-church.org.uk/index.shtml, tel. 01242 524889) was built in 1846 on the site of an earlier chapel and is a good example of the 'incorrect Gothic' style that was characteristic of similar early nineteenth-century Nonconformist chapels. Its early history can be told through the stone carving of a head to the left of the entrance. This is thought to be John Rattenbury, a twenty-two-year-old preacher, who held an outdoor service in 1828 from the steps of a house in St Philip's Street, just around the corner from the present building. After this event, the congregation started to grow quickly, and a disused blacksmith's shop was temporarily converted into a makeshift chapel until the present building was opened in 1846, with Rattenbury serving as its Wesleyan Methodist minister.

🦶 Retrace your steps back along Great Norwood Street. Then turn right into Suffolk Road and left into Bath Road.

Notice Cheltenham College Chapel (10) with its 'glorious soaring architecture' on your right.

It was designed by H. A. Prothero and built in 1896.

🐾 **Continue down Bath Road. Turn right and then left into College Road.**

At the junction with St Luke's Road you'll find St Luke's church (**11**) on your left.

An example of one of the stone carvings in St Luke's church.

★ St Luke's Church

St Luke's church (www.stlukes-church. org.uk), which was built in 1854 on a site purchased by Francis Close, was built partly as a chapel for Cheltenham College. It was designed by London architect Frederick Ordish in the Victorian 'Geometric Decorated Gothic' style. Its oddly shaped spire, described in one architectural guide as 'broached by ugly fat broaches', may be explained by the fact that its tower was originally intended to be 40 feet higher. Inside, there are many fine details, including window traceries, stained-glass windows, mosaics and carvings of angels and bishops.

🐾 **Proceed along College Road, and then continue into Hewlett Road. At the roundabout take the second exit into All Saints' Road.**

You'll find All Saints' church (**12**) on your right.

★ All Saints' Church

All Saints' church (www.allsaintschelt.net) was consecrated in 1868. A Grade I listed building, it is the most impressive of several buildings in the town designed by the local architect John Middleton (1820–85). Built in French Gothic style, its breathtaking interior includes a rose window in the south transept designed by Edward Burne-Jones (1833–98), as well as other features inspired by the Arts and Crafts movement. Its long association with music and the Holst family in particular (see walk 7) is also of great interest.

🐾 **Return back along All Saints' Road and at the roundabout, take the fourth exit into Fairview Road. Turn left into Winchcombe Street and then right into Albion Street.**

Immediately on your left is a short alleyway. This was one of the entrances that led to the Corn Exchange (**13**).

★ The Corn Exchange

It was on this site in 1864 that the social reformer George Jacob Holyoake (1817–1906) intended to deliver a lecture on 'The Changes of Religious Opinion in England since 1841'. However, he was barred from lecturing here because of his earlier imprisonment for blasphemy (see below). In fact, the lord of the manor arranged for the gas to be cut off at the Corn Exchange and also intimidated the owners of the other halls to prevent him from using alternative venues. Eventually, Holyoake delivered his lecture in a local inn.

🦶 **Continue along Albion Street until you reach the back entrance to Marks & Spencer.**
This is the site of the Mechanics Institute (**14**) and is located directly opposite the Pate's Almshouses, built as shown by the inscription on its façade in 1811.

★ **Mechanics Institute**
A chapel was built on this site in 1723, but by 1825 it had fallen into disrepair. The chapel was later demolished and the Mechanics Institute, established in 1834 to spread 'knowledge among the trading and mechanical portions' of the town, was built to replace it. Here, on 24 May 1842, George Holyoake gave a lecture on 'Home Colonisation as a Means of Superseding Poor Laws and Emigration', after which he became the last person in England to be imprisoned for denying the existence of God. Commenting in response to a question about the place of religion in socialist communities, he said, 'If poor men cost the state as much they would be put like officers upon half-pay, and while our distress lasts I think it would be wise to do the same thing with deity ... Morality I regard, but I do not believe there is such a thing as God.' Accused of blasphemy for these remarks, Holyoake returned to the Mechanics Institute on 2 June to defend his views at a meeting on free speech, but was arrested. At his trial he defended himself with a nine-hour speech, which could have been summarised more succinctly as 'Christianity says we are all brethren, but I like not that equality which allows one man to revel in his opinions – while others are punished with imprisonment in gaol for thinking theirs.' He was convicted for blasphemy and sentenced to six months in Gloucester gaol. Later, he coined the word 'secularism', which he defined as a concern with problems of this world, since he considered that the term 'atheism' was a less useful concept given its negative connotations.

🦶 Continue along Albion Street and turn right into Portland Street.
You will pass the Masonic hall (see walk 8) on your left.
🦶 Continue along Portland Street. Turn left and then third left into Bennington Street.

★ **Bennington Street**
Bennington Street has been described as 'the centre for [Cheltenham's] alternative spirituality'. Not only is its spiritualist church (www.snu.org.uk/community/churches/cheltenham. html, tel. 01242 511866) to be found here, but also No. 14 is the house where William G. Gray (1913–92), one of the twentieth century's most influential occultists, used to live. Gray ran a chiropody practice in the main shop floor, while his basement was arranged as his magical temple. It was also here he wrote some of his books, including *The Ladder of Lights* (1968) and *Magical Ritual Methods* (1971).

🦶 **Continue to the end of Bennington Street. Turn right for a few metres before turning left into the alleyway to return to Cheltenham Minster (St Mary's).**

Walk 5
Through the Looking Glass

Distance: 3.5 miles (2 miles without optional spur to Detmore)

Minimum Time: 2 hours (1 hour 15 mins for shortened walk)

Parking: Free car park in Church Piece.

Where to Eat and Drink: The Royal at 54 Horsefair Street, The Coffee Bean at 41 Lyefield Road West, King's Coffee House at 40 Church Street, and The Merryfellow at 2 School Road.

Where to stay: At Detmore House (Tel. 01242 582868, www.detmorehouse.com) you can stay at the house where the novelist Dinah Craik stayed while visiting the poet Sydney Dobell. The house is portrayed as Longfield in Craik's novel *John Halifax, Gentleman*.

Wraxall House, the home of the author Sir Nathaniel Wraxall, who called it his 'chateau'.

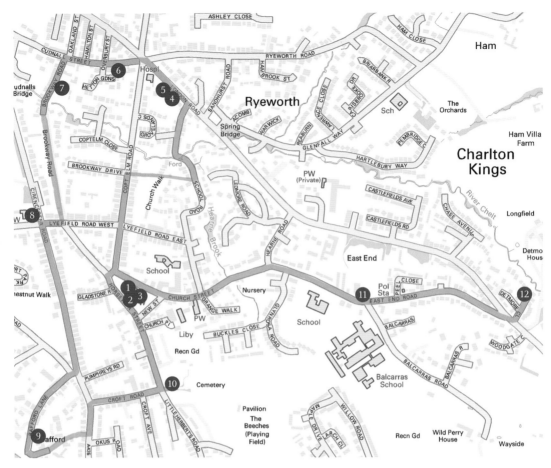

1. St Mary's church
2. Burns' memorial
3. Liddell memorial
4. Porturet House

5. The Grove House
6. Hetton Lawn
7. Wraxall House
8. Charlton Park Gates

9. Box Cottage
10. 'Tailor of Gloucester' memorial
11. Rear entrance of East Court
12. Detmore House

Over the years a wide range of poets and writers have visited or resided in Charlton Kings, one of Cheltenham's most attractive suburbs, which still retains its own separate identity and atmosphere. In particular, the Revd Charles Dodgson (1832–98), better known as Lewis Carroll, met his Alice here, drawing on this experience to develop a second book of *Through the Looking Glass* adventures. It was in 1863 that Dodgson visited the Revd and Mrs Henry Liddell at Hetton Lawn, Cudnall Street. Alice Liddell, who was holidaying with her sisters at their grandparents' house at the time, originally inspired Carroll to write *Alice's Adventures in Wonderland* (1865). It was during this visit that Carroll first saw a famous ornate mirror at Hetton Lawn which, it is believed, later inspired him to write the sequel, *Through the Looking Glass* (1871). It is also thought that the visit provided further inspiration for the book – when Dodgson took the three Liddell girls for a walk on Leckhampton Hill, they looked down on the Severn Vale countryside, which appeared, as described in *Wonderland*, 'marked out just like a giant chess board'. Also accompanying them on the walk was Miss Prickett, the governess for the Liddell children, who, according to Carroll, was the prototype for the Red Queen, 'the concentrated essence of all governesses!'

This walk explores Charlton Kings' rich literary heritage, from household names such as Dinah Craik and C. Day-Lewis to less well-known writers such as First World War poet Eva Dobell, or the more obscure 'rhymer' Isaac Bell, who was heavily influenced by Robert Burns. It also includes other literary connections of interest, such as the visit by John Byng, the 'chateau' that belonged to the memoirist, Sir Nathaniel Wraxall, and the real-life inspiration behind Beatrix Potter's *The Tailor of Gloucester* (1903).

This walk may be combined with the Cheltenham literary walk 'From Elysium to Hell' to make an all-day excursion. To do this, connect from site 6 on this walk to site 13 on walk 3. Allow twenty minutes one-way to do this by turning left at the top of Cudnall Street and walking down London Road.

★ St Mary's

The walk starts at the medieval church of St Mary's (**1**) which, among other items of interest, has a wonderful rose window, originally installed in 1824. Although the church was mostly rebuilt in 1877–8, the church dates back to 1190, when it was dedicated by William, Bishop of Hereford, as a chapel of ease to St Mary's, Cheltenham, now known as Cheltenham Minster. The church itself has several literary associations, including the fact that the bibliophile Sir Thomas Phillipps (see walk 3) married his first wife, Harriett Molyneux, here on 23 February 1819. Two more important links are to be found in the churchyard: not only is there an impressive memorial to Robert Burns' granddaughters, Sarah and Annie Burns, and his great-granddaughter, Margaret Constance Burns Hutchinson, who died between 1909 and 1925, but also the graves of the grandparents of 'Alice in Wonderland' are to be found here.

Enter the churchyard through the entrance from New Street.
Approximately 35 metres along the path on your right you'll find the Burns' memorial (**2**). The poet's two sons, Lieutenant Colonel William Nicol Burns and Major James Glencairn Burns, had moved to Cheltenham in 1846 in retirement after military service in India. Both became well-known figures in local social and public circles. The memorial includes the last verse from Burns' prayer 'O Thou Dread Power' (1786): 'When, soon or late, they reach that coast, / O'er life's rough ocean driven, / May they rejoice, no wand'rer lost, / A family in Heaven!'
Continue 14 metres towards the church.
On the left, between two cross-bearing memorials to John Phillips and John Gregson Harrison M.D., is the memorial to Henry George Liddell (1787–1872) and his wife Charlotte, the grandparents of 'Alice in Wonderland' (**3**).
Continue on the path and turn right to exit from the church via Church Street. Turn left and then right into Copt Elm Road.
The name of the road derives from a freehold, Cops Elm, which was conveyed to John Copp in 1391. By 1905 the Cheltenham and District Light Railway operated electric trams along here.
On your left, at the junction with Lyefield Road West, you can stop for a drink at The Coffee Bean café.
Continue down Copt Elm Road and turn right along the footpath directly opposite Brookway Drive. Turn left on Church Walk and cross the bridge.
This is known as Spring Bottom on account of the public spring here. It was also here that Charlton Mill once stood, dating back to the fourteenth century and still in operation in the 1890s.

👣 **Continue ahead and walk uphill along School Road.**
Look back to see fine views of Leckhampton Hill.
👣 **Turn left into London Road.**
The first house on your left, at No. 243, is Porturet House (**4**).

★ **Porturet House**
Porturet House was once the home of the artist William Rivière (1806–76), who exhibited at the Royal Academy as a historical painter from 1826 and was a drawing master at Cheltenham College. His son, Briton Rivière (1840–1920), also lived here. He also attended Cheltenham College and, like his father, became an accomplished artist, exhibiting at the Academy from 1858. Briton Rivière achieved immense popularity with the Victorian public through his paintings of animals. Of local interest, apart from the works contained at The Wilson, Cheltenham Art Gallery & Museum, are the sketches of pigs from East End farm in Charlton Kings, which he used in the painting entitled *Circe and the Swine*, as well as the painting of husky dogs, which he contributed to his son Hugh's life-size portrait of the Antarctic explorer Edward Wilson (see walk 6), which hangs in Cheltenham College. Also of interest is the fact that in 1867 Briton Rivière married Mary Alice Dobell of Detmore, a sister of the poet Sydney Dobell (see below), who died in 1874.

👣 **Continue towards 'Six Ways'.**
At No. 239 (to the left of The Old Stables which is at No. 239a) is The Grove House (**5**), which is set well back and hidden behind some conifers.

★ **The Grove**
This was the house where the poet Eva Dobell (1876–1963), niece of Sydney Dobell (see below), was born. She was best known for her poems inspired by her experience as a Voluntary Aid Detachment (VAD) nurse during the First World War. One of her most famous poems, entitled 'Pluck' (1916), begins, 'Crippled for life at seventeen, / His great eyes seem to question why: / With both legs smashed it might have been / Better in that grim trench to die / Than drag maimed years out helplessly.'

👣 **At 'Six Ways' turn left into Cudnall Street.**
On the corner with Hetton Gardens you'll find Hetton Lawn (**6**). The house is best viewed from Hetton Gardens.

★ Hetton Lawn
This house, formerly known as Bolton House, was built in 1862 and became the retirement home of Revd Henry George Liddell and his wife Charlotte, who came from Hetton-le-Hole, County Durham. The ornate mirror, with its figures of a shepherd, shepherdess, birds and nests, is located today on the landing, but when their granddaughter Alice stayed at the house in 1863 it was situated above the fireplace in the drawing room with its tall windows, reflecting the garden. Charles Dodgson became a friend of the Liddells through Henry and Charlotte's son, who, like his father, was also known as Revd Henry George Liddell (1811–98). The latter, who later became a famous lexicographer, was also Dean of Christ Church College in Oxford, which is where he first met Dodgson.

🐾 **Continue down Cudnall Street.**

Notice Elborough Cottage at No. 36 on your left, which is said to be the place the Wraxall family (see below) stayed while their house was being built.

🐾 **Turn left into Brookway Road.**

Brookway Road, once known as Stews Lane because of the Stewe family who resided here in the sixteenth century, is so named because it crosses the River Chelt.

Approximately 100 metres along the road on your left, passing the impressive villas called Courland (built *c.* 1830) and Hamilton House (built *c.* 1805–10), at No. 15 you'll find Wraxall House (**7**). Directly opposite here, at 26 Brookway Road, is the house where, until 2012, the journalist and writer Cressida Connolly, daughter of writer Cyril Connolly (1903–74), lived.

★ **Wraxall House**

Wraxall House was built in 1816 for the author of travelogues and historical memoirs Sir Nathaniel Wraxall (1751–1831), who referred to it as his 'chateau'. Wraxall became famous for his collection of memoirs covering political intrigue, especially in European diplomatic and royal circles, and life in London, where the character and physiognomy of the people that

he encountered were captured in amusing detail. Of particular local interest is the fact that his memoirs make brief mention of Lord Fauconberg, who made his house available to the royal party during George III's visit in 1788. Wraxall commented that being 'constitutionally subject to a violent scorbutic humour in his face, he [Lord Fauconberg] had recourse to the mineral waters of Cheltenham'. His memoirs also provide valuable details about George III's visit: 'He [George III] visited the [Cheltenham] spring at so early an hour, that few of his subjects were found there to meet him. Constantly on horseback, when the weather permitted, from eleven to three, he sat down at four to dinner; strolled out like a citizen with his wife and daughters, on the public walk

The ornate mirror at Hetton Lawn, which partly inspired Lewis Carroll to write *Through the Looking Glass*.

soon after seven; and by eleven at night, everything was as completely hushed at Bays Hill Lodge as in a farmhouse.'

🦶 **Continue along Brookway Road, which becomes a path.**
The River Chelt is crossed at the point where the road ends and the path begins.
🦶 **At the end of the path turn right into Lyefield Road West.**
This road was cut in 1900 and after 1905 formed part of a tram route.
🦶 **Cross over at the traffic lights and turn right into Cirencester Road.**
On your left you'll soon see the entrance gates to Charlton Park (**8**), with its pillars adorned with eagles.

★ **Charlton Park**
This was one of the places that the diarist John Byng (1743–1813) visited during his extensive travels on horseback throughout England and Wales between 1781 and 1794. 'In the evening,' he wrote in *The Torrington Diaries*, 'I rode out and was soon driven back by the rain, but not before I had gone thro' some pleasant lanes, and cross'd several pastoral streams in the village of Charlton, 1 mile distant; near which is a neat house, belonging to Mr Prin, with a small deer park, and in a dry clean soil, which is a rarity abt Cheltenham.' The house mentioned by Byng, which now forms part of St Edward's School, was built in 1701 on the site of an earlier timber-framed house that was constructed around 1562–8. In 1788 George III was entertained here during his visit to Cheltenham. A bird's-eye view of the house and the grounds can be seen in a painting of 1748 by Thomas Robbins in The Wilson.

🦶 **Return to the traffic lights and continue along Cirencester Road.**
Cirencester Road was cut in 1825–6 as a new turnpike road. However, its residential development didn't take place until the end of the nineteenth century.
🦶 **Take second right into Newcourt Road and then immediately left into Bafford Lane.**
Towards the end of the lane on your left you'll find Box Cottage (**9**), neatly enclosed by a box hedge.

★ **Box Cottage**
Box Cottage was the home of Irish-born Poet Laureate Cecil Day-Lewis (1904–72), who moved to Cheltenham in April 1930 after being appointed as a master at Cheltenham College. A blue plaque to the right of the door records that the poet laureate lived here from 1933 to 1938. Originally consisting of five separate cottages which in part may date from the late seventeenth century, Box Cottage was partially concealed behind a large box hedge, making it look like 'a sequestered, escapist kind of house for one of the new come-down-out-of-that-ivory-tower poets'. The house itself became inspiration for Day-Lewis's poetry, providing the subject for 'Moving In', which was published in *A Time to Dance* (1935). It also became an important meeting place for visiting poets and writers. Among the most frequent of these was W. H. Auden, who at the time lived nearby in Malvern, and who would bed himself down in Box Cottage under layers of thick coats and blankets together with a copious supply of bananas to sustain him through their intense discussions and criticism of each other's work. Significantly, it was when the cottage roof needed to be repaired that Day-Lewis was provided

Box Cottage, the home of C. Day-Lewis from 1933 to 1938, as well as an important meeting place for visiting poets such as W. H. Auden.

with the stimulus he needed to enter the detective genre. The result was *A Question of Proof* (1935), which was the first in a series of twenty-three highly successful novels featuring the detective Nigel Strangeways, written under the pseudonym of Nicholas Blake.

👣 **Continue to the end of the lane as it bends to the left and take the narrow footpath between two wooden fences.**
Bafford Lane takes its name from 'Babba's ford' and refers to the crossing that once existed through the Lilley Brook at the bottom of the lane.
👣 **Turn left into Cirencester Road and then right into Croft Road.**
Croft Road was formerly known as Blind Lane, perhaps because its raised hump makes it impossible to see from one end to the other.
👣 **Cross over Horsefair Street and enter Charlton Kings cemetery.**
The cemetery is open from 1 April to 30 September, 9 a. m. – 7.30 p.m., and from 1 October to 31 March, 9 a.m. – 4.30 p.m. After entering through the lychgate, turn right and walk along the path for approximately 30 metres. Then take the first path on the left. Some 5 metres along from the corner of this block, i.e. the second grave in on the second row of graves, you'll find the grave of John Samuel Pritchard (1877–1934) (**10**).

★ The 'Tailor of Gloucester'
As the inscription on the memorial indicates, John Pritchard was the real 'Tailor of Gloucester' upon whom Beatrix Potter based her famous children's story. Beatrix's cousin told her the story of Pritchard, who owned a shop at 45 Westgate Street in Gloucester and had been

commissioned to make a suit for the new mayor by the end of the week. However, when he came to work on Monday morning he found that the suit had been miraculously finished apart from one button hole, which had a note attached to it that read, 'No more twist'. In fact, Pritchard's assistants had finished the suit themselves, having gone out on Saturday night and then returned to sleep in the shop, continuing the work on Sunday to pass the time because they didn't want to be seen in a dishevelled state by churchgoers. Pritchard encouraged the local legend that it had been the work of fairies, and even advertised himself as the tailor whose 'waistcoats are made at night by fairies'.

🐾 **Return to Horsefair Street and turn right.**
Once forming part of Hollow Lane, which dates back to the twelfth century, the present name of Horsefair Street is believed to derive from the time when horses were traded near the present war memorial.
🐾 **You can stop to eat or drink at The Royal.**
This historic pub overlooks St Mary's church.
🐾 **Arrive back at the church.**
The circular part of the walk finishes at this point. Now, you can either finish the walk here or continue to include the spur to East Court and Detmore.
🐾 **To continue, turn right into New Street and right again into Church Street.**
Church Street was previously known as Charlton Street or Crab End Way and follows the line of a twelfth-century lane.
🐾 **You can stop here for food or drink.**
On your right you'll find King's Coffee House and, on your left, The Merryfellow.
🐾 **Continue along Church Street, which then becomes East End Road.**
Before you enter this road notice the impressive villa known as The Hearne, situated at the corner with Hearne Road, which was built around 1828–32 in Tudor Gothic style. Continuing on, opposite and just beyond the entrance to Balcarras School, on your left, you'll see the rear entrance of East Court (**11**), a large house built by Richard Pruen between 1805 and 1811. This house was built on the site of an earlier house called Nether House, but unlike its predecessor, which solely faced East End Road, East Court was built with a carriage drive linking it to London Road.

★ **East Court**
East Court has now been converted into flats. However, between 1825 and 1833 this was the place where Isaac Bell, one of Cheltenham's most colourful poets, worked as a gardener. Bell, who was born at the beginning of the nineteenth century, described himself as 'just a Rhymer' who spent 'the days in gard'ning and the nights in rhyme'. He was well educated; he read, for example, Scott and Shenstone, and was particularly influenced by Robert Burns. The subjects for his poems ranged from observations of nature to political or historical events, although he is probably best remembered for his portrayal of local characters in Cheltenham such as the Charlton Kings man whom he described as 'a swearing, blustering sot, / Whose greatest pleasure was his pipe and pot, / With drink ne'er satisfied, whate'er he got', or the man who sold his wife in Gloucester market for eighteen pence, a quart of ale, and a pipe of tobacco! Bell was happily employed at East Court. In fact, East Court itself became the subject of one of his poems: a place, he wrote, where he lived 'contented / Both happy and free'.

🐾 **At the end of East End Road cross over and turn right into London Road.**
You will see a signpost on your left marked 'Detmore Longfield', which is next to a private road. Follow this road for some way to reach Detmore (**12**), which today is run as a bed and breakfast.

★ Detmore

Detmore was the house where the novelist Dinah Craik stayed while visiting the poet Sydney Dobell (1824–74) in 1853, shortly after she began writing *John Halifax, Gentleman*. When the novel was published four years later, Cheltenham was portrayed as Coltham, a place 'which then, patronized by royalty, rivalled even Bath in its fashion and folly'. Craik took this name from Coltham Lane (now Hales Road), which formed part of the Cheltenham/Charlton Kings boundary. Detmore itself appears in the novel as a house called Longfield: 'Longfield, happy Longfield! Little nest of love, and joy, and peace – where the children grew up and we grew old …' The poet Eva Dobell also recorded Craik's inspiration with Detmore through her poem entitled 'Longfield', which starts 'Do you know "Longfield"? She who wrote the book, / "John Halifax", has drawn it as his home: / "The long, low, creeper-covered house" she writes. / That's very true! Great purple clematis, / And white Montana scramble to the roof …' Her uncle Sydney Dobell was also greatly inspired by living in the rural environment of Charlton Kings. In one of his most heartfelt letters he wrote, 'I can write … under the necessity of the case here in London but every breath of inspiration is of Charlton air.'

🐾 **To finish the walk retrace your steps back to St Mary's church.**

Detmore, the house portrayed as Longfield in Dinah Craik's novel *John Halifax, Gentleman*.

Walk 6

Cheltenham in Antarctica

Distance: 3 miles

Minimum Time: 2 hours

Parking: Chester Walk (nearest) or Cheltenham Walk (located near Jessop Avenue).

Where to Eat and Drink: At start/end of walk: The Wilson Café at the museum in Clarence Street. Near the Cheltenham College section of the walk is Moran's Eating House at 123–129 Bath Road.

Where to stay: The George Hotel (www.stayatthegeorge.co.uk, tel.: 01242 235751) on St George's Road is only a few hundred metres from the Wilson statue.

The Wilson statue on The Promenade, sculpted by Lady Scott.

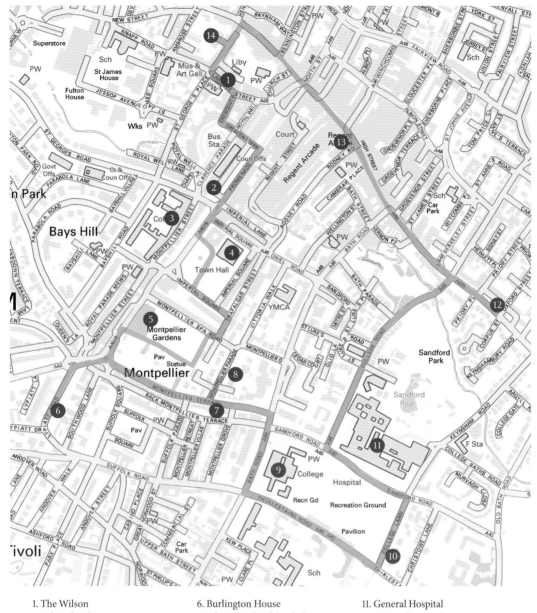

1. The Wilson
2. Edward Wilson statue
3. Cheltenham Ladies' College
4. Town Hall
5. Montpellier Gardens

6. Burlington House
7. Edward Wilson's birthplace
8. Site of Westal
9. Cheltenham College
10. Queen's House

11. General Hospital
12. 24 London Road
13. Site of the Assembly Rooms
14. 6 Jenner Walk

This walk explores Cheltenham's connections with Antarctic exploration, principally through one of its most famous sons, Edward Wilson (1872–1912), who perished with Captain Robert Scott (1868–1912) at the South Pole. Edward Wilson, or Ted, as he was generally known, was a doctor, scientist, naturalist and artist, and a leading member of Scott's *Discovery* (1901–4) and *Terra Nova* (1910–12) expeditions. He undertook important scientific work and was perhaps the last great practitioner of exploration art. He was one of the five men who reached the South Pole on 17 January 1912, only to discover that the Norwegian Roald Amundsen had arrived there five weeks earlier. During the return journey, Edgar Evans (1876–1912) and Lawrence Oates (1880–1912) fell ill and died, and later, around 29 March, Wilson, Henry 'Birdie' Bowers (1883–1912) and Scott perished in their blizzard-blown tent, only 11 miles from their next food depot.

In addition to this walk, there are other Wilson walks, which are included in chapter 12 of the book *Cheltenham in Antarctica* (Reardon, 2000). Of particular interest is a 2.5-mile walk which starts from the Wilson family's grave at St Peter's church, Leckhampton, and then leads to The Crippetts, a farm once rented by the family near the top of Shurdington Hill and which Wilson described as 'a little piece of heaven'.

🐾 **The walk starts at The Wilson (1), Cheltenham's Art Gallery & Museum in Clarence Street.** It is open daily from 9.30 a.m. to 5.15 p.m.

★ **The Wilson**
This is home to the Wilson Family collection. On the second floor a small gallery provides a display of artefacts, documents and photographs associated with the *Discovery* and *Terra Nova* expeditions. Among these are three Adélie penguins and other scientific specimens from the *Discovery* collections brought back in 1904, Wilson's pocket watch and the prayer book used by Surgeon Atkinson to read the burial service over the bodies of Scott, Wilson and Bowers on the Ross Ice Shelf in 1913. The display also includes another book that Wilson took with him to the Pole, a copy (annotated with his margin notes) of *Letters* by Samuel Rutherford, the seventeenth-century Scottish theologian and preacher. There is also an ever-changing display of Wilson's drawings and watercolours and other artefacts from the Wilson family collection as part of the museum's 'Paper Store' gallery.

It was Ted's father, Dr Edward Thomas Wilson (1832–1918), who was instrumental in establishing the museum. In 1891 he put forward proposals for 'A Museum for Cheltenham' and sixteen years later his hopes were realised when he officiated at its formal opening. When some of Wilson's paintings were exhibited here in 1914, the opening hours had to be extended until ten o'clock at night to cope with the huge number of visitors.

🐾 **Turn left after leaving the museum and then right into Crescent Place. Turn left and proceed to the end of Crescent Terrace, then turn right into The Promenade.**
The Promenade was described as 'the most beautiful, because the most verdant, of English streets' in Edward Thomas Wilson's 1901 guide to Cheltenham. At No. 92, currently occupied by Laura Ashley, there was a branch of W. H. Smith and Son's that contained an art gallery, which once displayed an exhibition of Herbert Ponting's photographs of the *Terra Nova* expedition.

★ **Statue**
Further along The Promenade, on the right-hand side, you'll find a bronze statue (**2**) of Wilson. This was sculpted by Lady Kathleen Scott (1878–1947), widow of Captain Scott, and unveiled by Sir Clements Markham, 'father' of the *Discovery* expedition, on 9 July 1914. It bears the following inscription:

Edward Adrian Wilson B.A. M.B. CANTAB. F.Z.S. Born in Cheltenham 1872. Chief of the Scientific Staff. Artist and Zoologist of the British Antarctic Expedition 1910–1913. He reached

the South Pole January 17, 1912. And died with Capt. Scott on the Great Ice Barrier March 1912.
He died as he lived. A brave true man. The best of comrades and staunchest of friends.

Letter from Capt. Scott

In front of the statue is one of three interpretation panels erected in 2012, the centenary of Wilson's reaching the Pole and death, depicting Wilson's life and achievements. Just around the corner from here, at 3 St George's Parade (part of St George's Place), is the house where the Cheltenham-born biographer the Revd George Seaver (1890–1976) stayed. It was his association with Cheltenham that initially brought him into contact with Wilson's sister, Ida, and later Wilson's widow, Oriana. Seaver wrote three biographical works on Wilson between 1933 and 1948, as well as biographies of Bowers (1938) and Scott (1940).

🐾 **Continue to the corner just beyond the Neptune fountain where The Promenade meets St George's Road.**
From here you can see, to the right, part of Cheltenham Ladies' College (**3**).

★ **Cheltenham Ladies' College**
The Ladies' College was the school that several of Wilson's sisters attended and of which his father was a governor. It also has several associations with polar exploration, including the fact that it houses a field telephone, which was donated by the father of one of the pupils, a director in the company that made it, and was used by the *Terra Nova* expedition for making some of the earliest telephone calls in the Antarctic. Another link with the Ladies' College is the fact that Glyngarth School – the first preparatory school that Wilson attended and where he learned Geography, English, History, Scripture, Latin, Mathematics and French, all the subjects necessary for him to progress to a public school – is now a boarding house for the college. Now called Farnley Lodge, the building can be seen in Douro Road, not far from Christ church.

🐾 **Cross over The Promenade, where you'll see the Town Hall (4) almost straight ahead.**

★ **Town Hall**
The Town Hall is a favourite place for lectures, and one that in the past has echoed to stories of Antarctic exploration, including those from Wilson himself (1906), from Captain Scott (1904) and Ernest Shackleton (1909, following his *Nimrod* expedition). More poignantly, Roald Amundsen gave a lecture about his successful polar conquest two months before the tragic news of the British expedition reached Cheltenham. Commander Edward 'Teddy' Evans (later Lord Mountevans of the Broke) lectured here on the tragedy in 1913, shortly after the expedition's return.

🐾 **Turn right up The Promenade. Then take the first path on the left to enter Imperial Gardens.**
Notice the statue of Gustav Holst (see walk 7).
🐾 **Cross Imperial Gardens to the corner diagonally opposite. Turn right and then right again into Montpellier Spa Road. Then turn left to enter Montpellier Gardens (5).**

★ Montpellier Gardens

Follow the path to the statue of William IV (see walk 9). While walking here it's interesting to consider that, even when Wilson was in Antarctica, he never forgot his Cheltenham home. Because his Antarctic diaries were written for the family he often made references to the town. It was his way of giving metaphorical access to the strange land and so, to some extent, to allow the family to share in his adventures. For example, on one occasion during the *Discovery* expedition when he accompanied Shackleton to take thermometer readings at the top of Crater Hill, he described the old volcanic cone at the top of the hill as being 'about as big as Montpellier Gardens'. However, while the average air temperature in Cheltenham would have been 9 °C, the temperatures on the top of Crater Hill, upon which incidentally Wilson would also sometimes stand and make sketches, were between -29°C and -40°C.

🐾 Turn right at the statue. You can stop here for a drink at the Garden Café.
🐾 Turn left into Montpellier Walk after exiting the park. Take the third exit at the roundabout and then turn left into Lypiatt Road.

Approximately 150 metres on your left, just before the road curves round to the left, is Burlington House (**6**).

★ Suffolk Hall School

Burlington House (formerly Suffolk Lawn) became the Suffolk Hall Preparatory School for boys during the second half of the nineteenth century. It was here that Wilson's future wife, Oriana Souper, or Ory for short, became a matron. Wilson made several visits here to see Ory and once stayed overnight, shortly before their wedding on 16 July 1901, as the guest of the James sisters who ran the school. Although Ted and Ory's happy marriage was cut tragically short, Ory overcame her husband's death partly through the outstanding services she provided to the New Zealand Red Cross during the First World War, which were later recognised through the award of a CBE. It is most appropriate, therefore, that Suffolk Hall itself was later converted into a Voluntary Aid Detachment (VAD) hospital from 1914 to 1919, a fact that is recorded on the panel displayed on the right-hand side of the porch.

🐾 Now retrace your steps back to the roundabout, this time taking the second exit into Montpellier Spa Road.

Along here on your right at No. 91, previously No. 6, is the house (**7**) where Wilson was born.

★ Birthplace

The four-storey house dates from before 1825. It was conveniently located for Ted's father, who worked as a physician at Cheltenham General Hospital. Ted was born in the front bedroom on the first floor in 1872, as the carved inscription on the façade indicates. In addition to a nursery on the top floor and a substantial kitchen in the basement there was accommodation for five servants.

🐾 Cross Montpellier Spa Road and turn left for approximately 50 metres and then right into Montpellier Parade.

On your right you'll find the entrance to the Eagle Tower car park (**8**), as well as the second of the three interpretation panels depicting Wilson's life and achievements.

Wilson's birthplace decorated with Union Jack pennant bunting during the 2012 Olympic Torch Relay.

★ Westal

This is the site of Westal, home to the Wilson family from 1874, when Ted was two, until the early 1930s. The house was one of three villas that were pulled down to make way for the 200-foot, thirty-storey Eagle Tower building. Described at the time as a 'superior villa' and 'desirable first-class detached family house', you can still appreciate how Westal would have looked from the surrounding villas that survive. The house took its name, which means 'west nook of land', from a small region located on the western side of Cheltenham. It was here that Ted's parents noticed that he was 'always drawing', leading them to encourage his artistic talent. It was also here that he developed some of his interest in nature, not only housing his ever-increasing natural history collections, but also occasionally providing a temporary home for his pets, including a buzzard he once brought back from Norway. Westal also became a focal point for visiting Antarctic explorers, including Captain Scott, whom Wilson's father described as 'clever, unassuming and amusing' when he stayed at Westal in December 1904. It was also the location for an important meeting that Ted arranged with Ernest Shackleton following concerns that Shackleton's proposed *Nimrod* expedition could interfere with Scott's future expedition plans.

🐾 Retrace your steps, turning left back into Montpellier Terrace. Then turn right into Bath Road.

Cross over and you'll see Cheltenham College (**9**) on your left, in front of which is the third of the interpretation panels.

★ Cheltenham College

This was the school that Wilson attended from 1886 for four years. In the College Chapel (not open to the public) there is the commemorative stained-glass 'Fortitude Window', one panel of which depicts Wilson as an Antarctic explorer. A memorial tablet, also in the chapel, has the following inscription:

> In memory of Edward Adrian Wilson, Physician, Zoologist, Artist, and Explorer, born 23rd July 1872, a member of this College from 1886 to 1891. A keen observer of

The 'Fortitude' window in Cheltenham College Chapel.

Nature. A wise and trusted friend. Gentle and God-fearing. Strong, simple, and sincere. He accompanied Captain Scott on both his Antarctic Expeditions; with him he reached the South Pole on 18th January, 1912; and with him he died on Ross Ice Barrier about March 27th, 1912.

There is also a memorial tablet to Ted's 'Uncle Charlie' – Major-General Sir Charles Wilson (1836–1905) – another old Cheltonian and a famous explorer in the Middle East.

Ted had fond memories of his old school and was later to return here to lecture on the *Discovery* expedition and also to give the occasional sermon. He shared an appreciation of the 'delicate tracery of the College chapel' with his father who, sleeping in his son's room at Westal on 17 December 1896, was suddenly awakened by a violent earthquake and later wondered how the College Chapel had withstood the strain while the pinnacles of Hereford Cathedral had been badly damaged.

🐾 **Continue along Bath Road and turn left into Thirlestaine Road, and then left again into College Lawn.** About 100 metres on your right is Queen's House (formerly Linden House) (**10**), now used as a girls' day house at Cheltenham College. This was also once the home of Ted's mother, Mary Agnes Wilson, *née* Whishaw (1841–1930).

★ **Mary Wilson**

The Whishaw family moved to Cheltenham around 1850, having founded one of the most successful Anglo-Russian trading companies. Mary, who was born in St Petersburg, was energetic and forthright. A good horse rider and a keen gardener, she also enjoyed painting, reading theological books, and was a respected authority on poultry farming. Following their wedding at St Luke's church, Ted's father noted that 'we adjourned to Linden House where the lawn was crowded with relations and friends'.

🐾 **Continue to the end of College Lawn and turn left into Sandford Road.**

Cross over and you'll soon see Cheltenham General Hospital (**11**) on your right.

★ **General Hospital**

In the summer of 1900, after Wilson qualified as a medical doctor, he worked briefly as a locum and then junior house surgeon at Cheltenham General Hospital, where he gave anaesthetics and performed minor surgery. Unfortunately, in the course of his medical duties he cut himself, and developed blood poisoning and an abscess of the axilla. He was then forced to resign from his post. Remarkably, however, a few months later, having recently had pus drained from his armpit, he went before the Antarctic committee with his arm still in a sling; although he was by no means fully fit, he was successfully recruited for the *Discovery* expedition.

🐾 **Continue along Sandford Road and turn right into College Road.**
As you walk along College Road notice St Luke's church (see also walk 4) on your left. This was the place where Ted's parents got married on 18 April 1865.
🐾 **At the end of College Road turn right and cross over to 24 London Road (12).**
Formerly 1 Priory Parade, this house, which is marked by a blue plaque, is where the botanical explorer and naval surgeon Dr David Lyall (1817–95), lived after retiring to Cheltenham.

★ **David Lyall**
A close friend of Ted's father, Lyall often gave thrilling accounts of his adventures as an explorer, including when he was medical officer and naturalist on Sir James Ross's *Erebus* and *Terror* expedition (1839–42), the first ever scientific expedition to the Antarctic. Lyall's stories undoubtedly contributed to Wilson senior's knowledge of the 'least explored portion of the globe' – Wilson gave a lecture on Antarctica in 1901 as President of Cheltenham Natural Science Society.

🐾 **Turn around and proceed back down London Road towards the town centre, continuing into the High Street.**
When you arrive at the corner with Rodney Road you'll see a Lloyds bank on your left. This is the site of the Assembly Rooms (**13**) (see also walk 3), which, as one of the main centres of fashionable society in Cheltenham in 1898, hosted a lecture by the Norwegian explorer Fridtjof Nansen (1861–1930) about his Arctic travels. This attracted over 3,000 people, including Ted's father, who later reflected, 'Little did we think that one day our dear Ted would be telling of his own adventures in the far South.'
🐾 **Continue down the High Street and, at the junction with St George's Place, turn left. Then take the second right into Jenner Walk.**
Along here on your left, you'll find No. 6, originally called 29, St George's Terrace (**14**).

★ **Emily Bowers**
This is the house where Emily Bowers (*née* Webb) (1847–1928), mother of Henry 'Birdie' Bowers, lived. She became a missionary teacher and her son, whom Scott described as 'a marvel', became one of Wilson's closest friends during the *Terra Nova* expedition. Emily was born in Cheltenham and was christened in St Mary's parish church, where the Revd Francis Close (see walk 4) was its long-serving curate. Her father, who ran a tailor's business, was one of the parishioners who signed a farewell scroll of thanks to Close when he left Cheltenham in 1856 to become Dean of Carlisle. Emily also attended two other institutions founded by Close: Holy Trinity School for Girls, located in Jersey Street, and the Anglican St Mary's teacher training college, originally located at 305–9 High Street.

🐾 **Return back along Jenner Walk. Then turn right into St George's Place and left into Clarence Street to return to The Wilson.**

Walk 7

From *Lansdown Castle* to *Egdon Heath*

Distance: 4.5 miles, but the walk may be reduced to 2.75 miles if the extension to Lansdown 'castle' is not included.

Minimum Time: 2 hours 50 mins (or 1 hour 40 mins if only town centre section included)

Parking: The Brewery car park on Monson Avenue is the most convenient.

Where to Eat and Drink: Towards the beginning and end of the walk, the following are most convenient: The Feathered Fish Bar and Kitchen at 104–6 Winchcombe Street; Joules Cafe, Bar & Restaurant at the Clarence Court Hotel, Clarence Square; and the Storyteller Restaurant & Wine Room at 11 North Place. In the centre of town, at 24 Rodney Road, you can visit Svea café and restaurant in recognition of Holst's Swedish ancestry.

Where to stay: Conveniently close to the Holst Birthplace Museum are The Cheltenham Townhouse Hotel at 12–14 Pittville Lawn (Tel. 01242 221922, www.cheltenhamtownhouse.com), and the Clarence Court Hotel in Clarence Square (Tel. 01242 580411, www.clarencecourthotel.com/index.php), which was once owned by the Duke of Wellington.

The interior of the Town Hall.

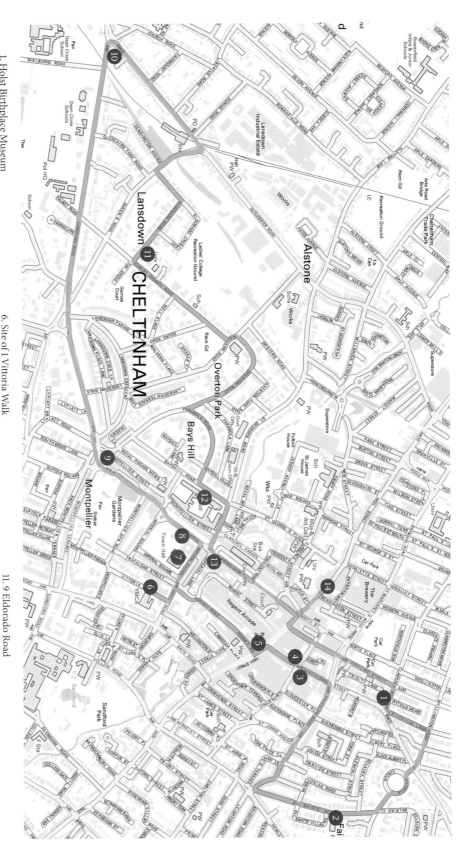

1. Holst Birthplace Museum
2. All Saints' church
3. Site of Highbury Congregational church
4. Site of the Corn Exchange
5. Site of the Assembly Rooms

6. Site of 1 Vittoria Walk
7. Town Hall
8. Holst statue
9. The Rotunda
10. Site of Lansdown 'castle'

11. 9 Eldorado Road
12. Cheltenham Ladies' College
13. Site of Dale, Forty & Co.'s music warehouse
14. Site of Cheltenham Grammar School

One of Cheltenham's most famous sons, the composer Gustav Holst (1874–1934), was himself a keen rambler. 'Walking,' he wrote, 'always sets me thinking of new tunes.' When he became part-time organist and choirmaster in the Cotswold village of Wyck Rissington as well as being conductor of the Bourton-on-the-Water choral society, he enjoyed walking the 20 miles home to Cheltenham. As a student at the Royal College of Music he thought nothing of walking, partly as a means to save money, the 97 miles from London to Cheltenham, sometimes even practising his trombone on the way, much to the astonishment of local farmers, who heard these impromptu performances and even claimed that the sounds induced pregnant sheep to go into early labour.

This walk celebrates the sites in the town which are associated with his life and music, including the places where he premiered his first operetta, *Lansdown Castle*, and the tone poem 'Egdon Heath' (1927), which, despite the international success and widespread popularity of *The Planets* (1914–16), he still considered to be his finest work. For those wishing to go farther afield, however, there is a medium-distance rambler's route from Cranham to Wyck Rissington via Cheltenham and Bourton described in *The Gustav Holst Way* (see www. holstmuseum.org.uk/gustav-holst-way.htm for further details).

As you walk, use your ears too. Holst drew some of his musical inspiration from the streets of Cheltenham, so you never know what you might hear in his music. When he came to compose his 'Toccata' for piano, for example, he based it on 'Newburn Lads', the Northumbrian pipe tune that he heard an old man with a hurdy-gurdy playing in 1879. Amusingly, he recalled that it was the only tune the man could play, and each time he played it there were fewer notes than before, to the extent that eventually the melody became barely recognisable.

The walk starts at the Holst Birthplace Museum (1) in Clarence Road.
This is open in February–May and October–mid-December from Tuesday to Saturday, 10 a.m. – 4 p.m., and in June–September from Tuesday to Saturday 10 a.m. –5 p.m., Sunday 1.30 p.m. – 5 p.m. (www.holstmuseum.org.uk).

★ Holst Birthplace Museum
Holst was born on 21 September 1874 at 4 Pittville Terrace (now Clarence Road) and lived there until the death of his mother in 1882. Originally built in 1832 as part of the Pittville estate, the small Regency house is now a museum and celebrates his life and work through temporary and permanent displays, which include the piano on which much of *The Planets*, his most celebrated work, was composed. The museum also has a 'Discovery Space' where visitors can 'turn the pages' of original Holst manuscripts, the majority of which date from when Holst attended Cheltenham Grammar School. Visitors can also hear recordings of each piece. The house also depicts the upstairs–downstairs life typical of Victorian and Edwardian households, while the living room has been furnished in the style of an 1830s room as it would have looked before the Holst family moved there, to convey the type of room in which Holst's grandfather Gustavus Valentine von Holst (1799–1871) would have given harp and piano tuition to Cheltenham's young ladies. Although not located in a very central part of town, the house also provided the young Holst with a memorable street-scene experience. Looking out from one of the front windows, he noticed a troupe of Morris men with blackened faces dancing outside. It was an incident which gave him a considerable fright, and was one he was to remember for the rest of his life.

🐾 After leaving the museum, turn right and cross Clarence Road.

You will then be opposite the recently restored gates which formed the original entrance to Pittville Park.

🐾 Go around the gates and enter Pittville Lawn. Then turn right into Wellington Road.

Like Pittville Terrace, Pittville Lawn also formed part of the original Pittville estate.

🐾 Take the third exit at the roundabout, then turn right at the mini roundabout into All Saints' Road.

All Saints' church (**2**) is approximately 200 metres along on your left.

★ All Saints' Church

The close associations between the Holst family and All Saints' go back to the church's foundation in 1867 when Holst's father became organist there, a panel inside the church recording his appointment as continuing until 1895. But it was also the place where Holst's parents were married on 11 July 1871 and where Gustav was christened on 21 October 1874. The church played an important part in Gustav's musical development. We know, for example, that at the age of four his father took him here and played a tune on the organ. He'd previously taught Gustav to play this on the piano at home, and when Gustav heard it he proclaimed loudly, 'That's my tune!' It was also here that he sang in the church choir, played violin or trombone in the church's small orchestral group and, through his father's position, he was able to practise the organ and try out his new compositions here, including 'Four Voluntaries', which he dedicated to his aunt Nina. Because of this association, the Holst Birthplace Museum regularly holds its Holst birthday concert here each year on or around 21 September, the date of Gustav's birth in 1874. This annual concert is firmly established in Cheltenham's musical calendar.

🐾 After leaving the church, turn left and then right at the mini roundabout into Fairview Road.

🐾 Then turn left at the junction with Winchcombe Street.

At the next junction on the corner of Winchcombe Street and Albion Street, you'll find an old art deco cinema, originally known as the Gaumont Palace, and later the Odeon, which was closed in 2006 and is currently under redevelopment. The Beatles appeared here in 1963, but previously it was the site of Highbury Congregational church (**3**), which was built in a Gothic Revival style in 1850–2. It was here on 8 May 1895 that, by way of celebrating his son's success in obtaining a scholarship for composition at the Royal College of Music,

The organ at All Saints' church.

Holst's father arranged a performance of Gustav's 'Duet' for organ and trombone. Adolph played the organ on this occasion, having recently retired as organist of All Saints' church.

🐾 **Cross Albion Street and then turn right, continue for 20 metres.**

On your left is a short alleyway. This was one of the entrances that led to the Corn Exchange (**4**); the other entrance that was previously useable was from the High Street, at approximately No. 165, which is currently occupied by the O2 phone shop, before further development took place.

★ **The Corn Exchange**

The Corn Exchange was converted from the Old Market House in 1863 and 'admirably adapted for Concerts, Lectures, Meetings and other Entertainments, having Orchestra and other convenient appendages'. On 7–9 February 1893 this was the venue for the first three complete performances of Holst's comic operetta *Lansdown Castle, or The Sorcerer of Tewkesbury*, with Gustav providing piano accompaniment. Although the audience was surprised to see such a young composer, which, as one critic commented, 'was suggestive either of unusual talent or of precarious mediocrity', they were won over by a performance described as 'remarkable and not unworthy of a trained and experienced musician'. Gustav's melodies were praised as 'always flowing, tuneful, expressive, and free from conventionality' and overall it was seen as 'proof of the possession of a very great and available talent'.

🐾 **Return to Winchcombe Street and turn right towards the town centre. Then turn left into the High Street.**

Approximately 40 metres along on your right, on the corner of the High Street and Rodney Road, you'll find the neo-Baroque building of a Lloyds bank, which was built on the site of the Assembly Rooms (**5**).

★ **The Assembly Rooms**

Opened in 1816 by the Duke and Duchess of Wellington, the Assembly Rooms formed an important part of Cheltenham's social centre. Apart from hosting concerts by famous musicians such as Niccolò Paganini (1782–1840), Johann Strauss (1804–49) and Franz Liszt (1811–86), it was also the place where Holst conducted some selections from *Lansdown Castle* on 22 December 1892. He later submitted the score with his application, albeit unsuccessful on this occasion, for a scholarship to the Royal College of Music.

🐾 **Turn right into Rodney Road, where there are several places to eat or drink.**

At No. 24 you can visit Svea, Cheltenham's only Swedish café and restaurant, in recognition of Holst's family, which was of Swedish origin.

🐾 **Proceed to the end of the road as it curves to the left. Cross over at the junction and turn left into Oriel Road and then take second right into Vittoria Walk.**

As you pass the telephone exchange on your right you'll see the site, now occupied by BT, of a grand villa that once stood here. This was 1 Vittoria Walk (**6**).

★ **1 Vittoria Walk**

This was the house to which the family moved in 1882 following the death of Holst's mother, Clara. Gustav was then eight. He and his younger brother Emil, who later became the

Hollywood actor Ernest Cossart, were then brought up by his aunt Nina, an accomplished pianist who had known Liszt, until his father married Mary Thorley Stone in 1885. She gave birth to two further sons, Matthias Ralph and Evelyn Thorley. By 1891 the family's neighbours reflected Cheltenham's growing importance as an educational centre. Wolseley House, the house to the right, which was demolished and replaced by the telephone exchange, was home to the headmaster of Cheltenham Grammar School, which Gustav attended from 1886 to 1891, while 2 Vittoria Walk, the neighbouring house (also demolished) on the left-hand side, was occupied by three assistant mistresses at Cheltenham Ladies' College.

🐾 **Return to Vittoria Walk and turn left into Oriel Road. Continue into Imperial Square.** On your left you'll see the Town Hall (**7**).

★ Town Hall
It was here on 27 March 1927 that Holst conducted *The Planets* as part of a festival of his music organised by the local council. After the concert, he was presented with a painting by Harold Cox, now on display in the Holst Birthplace Museum, that depicted the positions of the planets, as calculated by the Astronomer Royal, which would have been visible from the top of Cleeve Hill on 25 May 1919, the date assumed to coincide with the first performance of *The Planets*. Holst described the festival as 'the most overwhelming event of my life'. In fact, he was so thrilled that he returned to the Town Hall the following year, this time to conduct the British premiere of his new work 'Egdon Heath', an atmospheric tone poem that depicts the heath portrayed in Thomas Hardy's novel *The Return of the Native* (1878). Holst included Hardy's description of the heath in the score: 'A place perfectly accordant with man's nature – neither ghastly, hateful, nor ugly; neither common-place, unmeaning nor tame; but, like man, slighted and enduring; and withal singularly colossal and mysterious in its swarthy monotony.' Holst considered this to be his finest work ever, and fittingly it formed Holst's last public performance in his native town.

🐾 **Continue to the end of Imperial Square and turn left into the Promenade.**
Then take the first path on the left to enter Imperial Gardens and visit the Holst statue (**8**), which stands aloft a fine memorial fountain.

★ Holst Statue
The statue was sculpted by Anthony Stones and unveiled on 4 April 2008 by the well-known Hallé Orchestra music director Sir Mark Elder. Notice that Holst, although right-handed, is holding the baton in his left hand. This is because he was often troubled with painful neuritis in his right hand. Notice also the seven plaques incorporated into the octagonal plinth below, which depict the planets. These are arranged in an astrological, not astronomical order. Holst intended the orchestral suite to deal with the 'seven influences of destiny and constituents of our spirit', and so arranged the planets in the following way, symbolising life's experiences and progression from youth to old age: Mars, the bringer of war; Venus, the bringer of peace; Mercury, the winged messenger; Jupiter, the bringer of jollity; Saturn, the bringer of old age; Uranus, the magician; and Neptune, the mystic.

Statue of Gustav Holst.

🐾 **Continue on The Promenade, which then joins Montpellier Walk.**
You'll pass the Queen's Hotel (see walk 2) on your left. Then before you reach the roundabout you'll arrive at the Rotunda (**9**) on your right.

★ **Rotunda**
A popular place for concerts before it became a Lloyds bank, it was probably here that Holst heard a chamber orchestra for the first time. His father often directed chamber orchestra concerts and gave piano recitals at this venue. In fact, when his father was a bachelor he offered music lessons just around the corner from here at 16 Rotunda Terrace. He also encouraged his son to attend rehearsals here, teaching him how to check parts and cue in missing instruments. This was a skill that he used to good effect in later life. The Rotunda was also the venue where the young Holst premiered several of his own compositions, including an intermezzo, which the *Cheltenham Looker-On* described as consisting of an 'opening movement with muted first violin, with pizzicato accompaniment, and a tuneful melody in second part for clarionet and flutes'. It commented further: 'The work was well received, and the youthful composer bowed his acknowledgements.' Later on, the Rotunda also witnessed the premiere of his 'Duet in D' for two pianos when it was performed here by father and son on 13 May 1899.

At this point you can either continue the walk to see two additional sites, i.e. the site of Lansdown 'castle', which gave its name to Holst's first operetta and the house where the international violinist Marie Hall lived, or you can return towards the town centre and complete the remaining sites. To do the latter, retrace your steps down Montpellier Walk and The Promenade, turning left at St George's Road, then second left into Bayshill Road to arrive at the Ladies' College (**12**).

🐾 **To continue, proceed along Montpellier Walk and turn right at the roundabout into Lansdown Road.**
Notice the magnificent villas which front Lansdown Road, including on your left some of the buildings which form part of Dean Close School, named after the Revd Francis Close (see walk 4).
🐾 **Continue until you reach the junction with Gloucester Road.**

★ **Lansdown 'Castle'**
Here, at the corner of Lansdown Road and Gloucester Road, you'll see the site of Lansdown 'castle' (**10**), which gave its name to Holst's first operetta, which he composed at eighteen. The original 'castle' was a rectangular two-storey crenellated building built in the 1850s, which was demolished in about 1972. The libretto was written by a local resident, Major A. C. Cunningham. Set in the reign of King Henry VII, it contained no real plot; rather it was a 'slender stringing together, in a whimsical way, of various incidents, more or less improbable'. Strongly influenced by Gilbert and Sullivan operas, it included lines – which Holst expertly set to music – such as, 'Lord Raymond cannot care / My tender heart to spare, / Or he would never dare / To give that beggar beef and beer. / Oh! Beef and Beer. / Forgive this tear (*weeping*) ... The men will jeer, the women sneer, / When told this tale of Beef and Beer.'

🐾 **Turn right into Gloucester Road. Then turn right into Queen's Road at the roundabout.**
You'll pass the railway station on your right. Opened in 1840, this was originally known as Lansdown station and was built with an imposing Doric portico which, unfortunately, was later removed.

🐾 **Turn left into Eldorado Road, which curves to the right.**
At Rosemead, 17 Eldorado Road, you'll pass the family home of Brian Jones (1942–69), founder of the Rolling Stones rock group (see walk 9). At Broadleas, 9 Eldorado Road (**11**) you'll find the house, now a rest home, where the international violinist Marie Hall (1884–1956) lived.

★ **Marie Hall**
Regarded as the finest British woman violinist of her age, she was the dedicatee of Holst's 'Valse Etude' as well as 'The Lark Ascending', which Holst's friend Vaughan Williams composed for her in 1914. In 1911 she married her manager, Edward Baring. The couple moved to Cheltenham, where they remained for the rest of their lives.

🐾 **Continue to the end of Eldorado Road and turn left into Christchurch Road.**
Christ church (see walk 4) provides a dramatic focal point in the road.
🐾 **Turn left at the church into Malvern Road, then right into Overton Road.**
Follow this road as it sweeps round to the right.
🐾 **Turn left into Parabola Road and left again into Bayshill Road.**
On the corner of these two roads you'll find a Victorian pillar box of the hexagonal Penfold type, one of eight in Cheltenham, and only ninety-four in the whole country.
🐾 **Cross over and immediately on your right you'll see Cheltenham Ladies' College (12).**

★ **Cheltenham Ladies' College**
Holst's grandfather became established as a music teacher in Cheltenham in the early 1850s, at the time when the social profile of the town was beginning to change, shifting from pleasure seeking at the spa towards evangelical preaching and learning as Cheltenham became an important centre for religion and education. In 1854 he was appointed as a music professor at the newly opened Ladies' College, which was then located in Cambray Place. Here he arranged public concerts for his pupils to perform on The Promenade. He adopted the practice of prefixing his surname with 'von' to sound more aristocratic and reinforce the belief that if you were a foreigner you were more likely to be a good musician. Holst followed this practice himself until it became a disadvantage to be perceived, albeit not mistakenly, as having Germanic origins during the First World War. It was also at the Ladies' College in the 1870s that Holst's father began teaching the piano and this was the place where he fell in love with, and subsequently married, Clara Cox Lediard (1841–82), one of his pupils.

🐾 **At the end of Bayshill Road turn right into St George's Road and then right into The Promenade.**
Situated opposite the Neptune Fountain and on the left, at the corner of The Promenade and Imperial Lane, where the fashion retailer Gap is currently located, was Dale, Forty & Co.'s music warehouse (**13**).

★ **Dale, Forty & Co.**
The building was a familiar sight on The Promenade and supplied the town with everything to do with music from the late 1870s until 1961. Behind the premises in Imperial Lane, the Dale,

The statue of Richard Pate at the school's current site in Princess Elizabeth Way.

Forty piano workshops imported, assembled and repaired pianos. The firm was co-founded by Cheltenham-born Frank Forty (1846–1916), himself an enthusiastic amateur musician, composer and fellow chorister at All Saints'. He was also Gustav's godfather, and his daughter Mabel, who had a strong, attractive personality, was a close friend of Gustav's. They often played duets together, and he even dedicated his 'Introduction and Bolero' for piano duet to her as his 'adored Beloved Sweet-Heart'. Frank Forty was convinced that Gustav was destined to become a great composer and strongly encouraged him. Although Dale, Forty & Co. is no longer a trading company, imported pianos bearing the 'Dale, Forty Cheltenham' name are still available from the Cheltenham Piano Centre at 52 Winchcombe Street.

👣 **Proceed along The Promenade and then turn left into the High Street at Boots Corner.** On your right at 252–3 High Street, outside the Wilkinson's store, you'll find a green civic society plaque marking the site of Cheltenham Grammar School (**14**).

★ Cheltenham Grammar School

Originally founded by Richard Pate (1516–88) in 1572 with a grant from Elizabeth I, Cheltenham Grammar School was rebuilt in 1887–9 before being relocated to its current site in Princess Elizabeth Way. Holst attended the school from 1886 to 1891, at a time when the school was being reconstructed, and so his education took place mainly in temporary accommodation. Holst was not particularly happy at school. This was perhaps because of the cramped conditions or perhaps because his asthma and short-sightedness prevented him from participating in more active pursuits with his fellow pupils. Inevitably, however, he played an active part in the school's music

scene, and it was probably here on 18 December 1890 that he gave his first public performance as a pianist, playing work by Mayer, Grieg and A. Burnett. School also provided inspiration for his music. For example, when he premiered a song entitled 'Die Spröde' at the Montpellier Rotunda in 1891, although on this occasion it was sung in English, Holst probably came across the original lines from Goethe, which he then set to music, from his German studies at school.

👣 **Return to Boots Corner. Continue along the High Street, then turn left into Pittville Street, which continues into Portland Street.** Notice the magnificent Masonic hall (see walk 8) on your left, which was built in 1823.
👣 **Turn right at the junction with Clarence Road to return to the Birthplace Museum on your right.**

Walk 8

Street and Tree

Distance: 6.5 miles. Alternatively, the walk may be completed in three or four sections, using Pittville Park, Montpellier Park, The Park and Sandford Park as separate focal points.

Minimum Time: 3 hours 45 mins

Parking: There is ample free parking at Pittville Pump Room.

Where to Eat and Drink: At Pittville Park the outdoor café in Central Cross Drive is open seven days a week throughout the year (8 a.m. – 6 p.m. Monday to Saturday, 9 a.m. – 6 p.m. Sunday). Blankets and cushions are provided in winter and picnic blankets in the summer. The Garden Café at Montpellier Gardens is open during the summer from 8.30 a.m. to 6 p.m. Monday to Friday, 9 a.m. – 6 p.m. Saturday and Sunday. If this is closed, Coffee & Co. at 7 Montpellier Terrace is one of several cafés in close proximity to the gardens. The Tivoli pub and restaurant at 34 Andover Road, and Sandford Park Alehouse at 20 High Street are the most convenient for the latter stages of the walk.

Where to stay: At the Cotswold Grange hotel in Pittville Circus Road (Tel. 01242 515119, www.cotswoldgrangehotel.co.uk) you'll find a most convenient and quiet tree-lined avenue location. At Clarence Court Hotel in Clarence Square (Tel. 01242 580411, www.clarencecourthotel.com/index.php) you can stay in a Regency building once owned by the Duke of Wellington. At the Queen's Hotel (Tel. 0118 971 4700, www.queenshotelcheltenham.com/index.htm) you'll be able to appreciate the most spectacular view of the tree-lined Promenade.

The bandstand at Pittville Park.

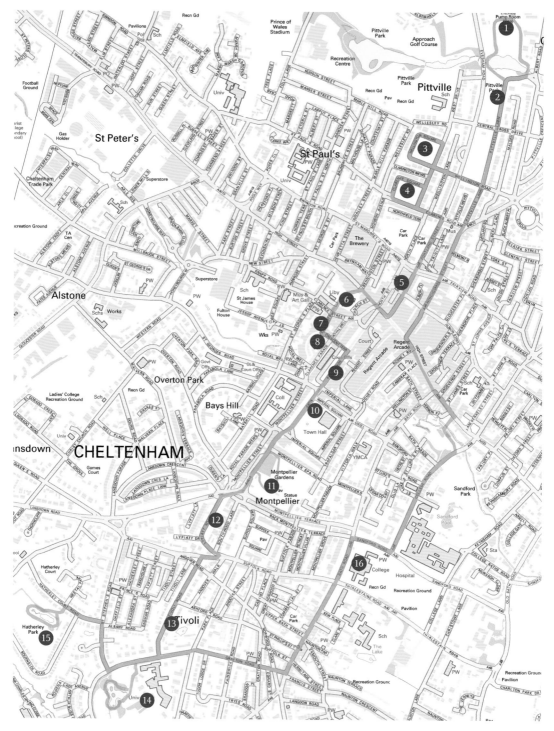

1. Pittville Park
2. Pittville Lawn
3. Wellington Square
4. Clarence Square
5. Masonic hall
6. Cheltenham Minster
7. John Dower House
8. Royal Crescent
9. The Promenade
10. Imperial Gardens
11. Montpellier Gardens
12. Lypiatt Road
13. Tivoli Road
14. The Park
15. Hatherley Park
16. Cheltenham College
17. Sandford Park

When the poet Lady Margaret Sackville (1881–1963), went to live in Cheltenham in 1936, she found one of the attractions of her new home was its arboreal beauty. Eleven years later, she published a poem entitled 'How the Trees Came to Cheltenham', in which she eulogised the town's 'perfect union' between 'street and tree'. In this 'fantasy' she recalled how Cheltenham's hope to have 'each spacious street ennobled by a tree' was happily fulfilled after the forest trees '... sorely lamed / By their long march, there settled down to grow ...' and then, at the poem's conclusion, she claimed that 'you'll find no place, search all the world who may, / So countrified, so urban and gay, / Or where in perfect union, wild yet free, / Live on an equal footing street and tree.'

In reality, Cheltenham's 'perfect union' with trees dates back to its development as a spa, when Captain Henry Skillicorne (1678–1763), its first developer, decided to plant forest trees within the town. In his diary he recorded, 'In the winter of 1739 I made the upper walk, planted elm and lime to the number of 37 ... To the winter of 1740 I made the lower walk, planted 96 elms at the expense of £56.' When considering what to plant, Skillicorne was influenced by the Regency ideal expressed in John Evelyn's *Sylva, or a Discourse of Forest-Trees* (1662), which advocated bringing the countryside into the town ('*rus in urbe*') and promoted the benefits of lime trees for street planting. Although it is unlikely that any of Skillicorne's original plantings have managed to survive, part of his lasting legacy is the beauty of Cheltenham's tree-lined avenues today and its verdant parks and gardens. However, with the constant threat from new pests and diseases, the town's population of trees exists in a fragile environment. In 1980 alone Dutch elm disease took toll of 4,500 trees in the town. Today, while Skillicorne would still be able to find hundreds of limes, he would struggle to find an equal number of healthy elms. Nevertheless, trees remain an important part of the town's heritage. With an estimated 60,000 specimens in total, there is roughly one tree for every two residents. Bearing this in mind, it is, therefore, well worth bringing a good tree guide to enable you to enjoy this walk to the full. Scientific names for the more unusual species have been included in the text.

🐾 The walk starts at Pittville Park (1).

★ Pittville Park
Here, more than 850 trees create a green oasis on the edge of the town. Two self-guided tree walks can be downloaded from www.cheltenham.gov.uk/trees, which help to locate some of the most significant specimens here. Starting from the Pump Room (open Monday–Saturday, 10 a.m. – 5.30 a.m. when not being used for a private function) there is a pleasant circular walk to the upper lake that takes in a wide variety of native and exotic species. Apart from the common oak there is also a fine domed turkey oak (*Quercus cerris*) and a holm oak which, together with a yew, are likely to date back to the 1820s when the park was opened. One of the special trees in the park, flanked by the holm oak and a Caucasian wing nut (*Pterocarya fraxinifolia*), is a 14-metre-high pencil cedar (*Juniperus virginiana*), which is officially the largest specimen in the UK. Approximately 25 metres from the pencil cedar, in the direction of the park's play area, is a sycamore with a plaque commemorating the conservationist Richard St Barbe Baker (1889–1982). Baker attended Cheltenham's Dean Close School, where he became interested in botany and forestry. Later he founded the Men of the Trees Society, now the International Tree Foundation, the activities of which have seen billions of trees planted throughout the world. Other notable specimens in this section of the walk include a

red flowering chestnut (*Aesculus X carnea*), a Persian ironwood (*Parrotia persica*), a tulip tree (*Liriodendron tulipifera*), a common alder, a London plane, a horse chestnut, a Himalayan birch (*Betula utilis var. Jacquemontii*) and a strawberry tree (*Arbutus unedo*).

🦶 **Leave the south-eastern edge of the upper lake and proceed along Pittville Lawn (2).**
As you leave the lake notice the impressive weeping silver lime (*Tilia tomentosa 'Petiolaris'*) located near the water's edge. This has been recognised in the *National Tree Register* as one of the finest specimens in the UK.

★ **Pittville Lawn**
Pittville Lawn, which stretches from the lake to Central Cross Drive, was one of the original pleasure gardens of Pittville estate when it was laid out in the mid-1820s. Many of the trees and shrubs in this area, including an impressive cedar of Lebanon (*Cedrus libani*), probably date from the 1890s when the estate transferred into public ownership. The yew was also planted in this period but, given that yew trees can live for more than 1,000 years, this is still a relatively young specimen. Other notable specimens include the maidenhair tree (*Ginkgo biloba*), 'Balsam Spire' poplar (*Populus trichocarpa x balsamifera*), paperbark maple (*Acer griseum*); Dawyck beech (*Fagus sylvatica 'Dawyck'*), American or black walnut (*Juglans nigra*); Liquidambar (*Liquidambar styraciflua*); red oak (*Quercus rubra*); holm oak; California incense cedar (*Calocedrus decurrens*), London plane and yellow buckeye chestnut (*Aesculus flava*).

🦶 **You can stop here for a drink at the outdoor café in Central Cross Drive.**
🦶 **Turn right into Wellington Road and then enter Wellington Square (3) on your right.**

★ **Wellington Square**
Wellington Square, one of the original squares that formed part of the Pittville estate, was built from the 1820s. Named after the 1st Duke of Wellington, who visited Cheltenham five times between 1805 and 1828, its charm lies in its varied architecture and attractive public garden containing many traditional as well as more exotic trees such as ornamental pear. Among the most interesting houses are Glenmore Lodge built in 1826–7 in classic Regency style, the red-brick Victorian villa called Eastholme facing it, and the row of terraced houses in Tudor Gothic style on the west side where, at No. 6, the celebrated Shakespearean actor William Charles Macready (1793–1873) lived from 1860 until his death. A statue believed to be of Macready is located on the upper façade. Macready was not only the leading actor of his day but also a close friend to Charles Dickens (see walk 3), who came to stay at his house when he came to Cheltenham to give public readings of his work. Macready, although retired, also gave readings and lectures in Cheltenham, which he considered had 'conveniences of all kinds equal those of London'.

🦶 **Exit the square at the southern end of West Drive and then enter Clarence Square (4).**

★ **Clarence Square**
Clarence Square, the second of the two squares which formed part of the Pittville Estate, was built from 1832. Named after the Duke of Clarence, who later became King William IV, its attractive features include a public garden with London plane, yews and holm oaks enclosed

Yew tree sculpture in Clarence Square.

by hedges, as well as terraces of stuccoed houses both in traditional classical and Tudor Gothic style. Of particular interest is No. 19, which was once the residence of Charles Sturt (1795–1869), the explorer of Australia, who retired to Cheltenham in 1853 to spend the remaining six years of his life. In the south-western corner of the public garden there is also an attractive sculpture carved from a dead yew.

👣 **Exit the square by turning left into Clarence Road. Then take the second right into Portland Road.**

Just before the junction with Albion Street, notice on your left, at 3 Portland Street, the house, now occupied by the Everest Indian restaurant, where Cheltenham's first historian, John Goding (1816–79) lived from 1835 to 1874. Directly opposite this is the magnificent Masonic hall (**5**), which was built in 1823 by George Underwood (1793–1829), the architect of many of Cheltenham's finest churches as well as its municipal offices. Outside London, it was the world's first purpose-built Masonic hall, and today has the distinction of being Cheltenham's oldest non-ecclesiastical public building still in use for the purpose for which it was originally designed. Notable local freemasons have included Dr Edward Jenner (1749–1823), the founder of the smallpox vaccination, and Sir George Dowty (1901–74), the aeronautical engineer.

👣 **Turn right into the High Street, then left into Church Street to arrive in the churchyard of Cheltenham Minster (St Mary's) (6).**

★ Cheltenham Minster

At the beginning of the nineteenth century St Mary's churchyard was described as 'the most beautiful in England, extending from East to West, about 300 feet, and rendered particularly agreeable by its walks being shaded by double rows of lime trees, which surround and cross it'. A local poet even immortalised the limes in the following verse: ''Twas the sweet and blessed Sabbath, God's own holy hallowed hour, / And the bells were softly chiming, in Saint Mary's time worn tower. / Hush'd was the voice of labour, no harsh sounds disturbed the air, / And the rows of stately lime trees bowed their heads as if in prayer!' Appropriately, the churchyard is still a quiet green haven, just seconds away from the noise and bustle of the High Street and, fittingly, limes still form the largest part of its green canopy.

Exit the churchyard via Well Walk. Turn right and then immediately left into Crescent Place.
On your right notice the magnificent royal coat of arms above the portico of John Dower House (**7**). Originally dating as a boarding house from 1820, it became known as the Clarence Hotel following a visit by the Duchess of Clarence in 1827. Later, she became a queen as the wife of William IV, hence the building's royal connection.
Proceed to the end of Crescent Place to view Royal Crescent (8) on your right.

★ Royal Crescent
One of the architectural treasures of Cheltenham, this block of Regency houses (see also walk 2) is partially secluded by some attractive silver birches as well as fine mature London planes, which not only help to screen out noise but also to absorb the pollution from the inner ring road and the coach station located here. Notice also the wealth of very fine ornamental ironwork, of which Cheltenham has some of the finest examples in the country.

Royal Crescent, one of the town's architectural treasures.

🦶 Turn left along Crescent Terrace. Then take second right into The Promenade (9).

★ The Promenade
As the town's most famous thoroughfare, the beauty of The Promenade is greatly enhanced by the large number of trees adorning its edges in single- and double-line plantings. Horse chestnuts were originally planted here in 1818 when the road was constructed. However, when a large bough fell in 1977, prompting concerns for safety, London planes were recommended as a replacement, especially since their open crowns would allow the town's architecture to be more easily visible. The planes also provided a home to a colony of rooks which, although diminished in recent years, still create a unique atmosphere for a town centre in early spring, as described by Gloucestershire poet Sheila Simmons: 'But in the middle of it all / high in the peeling plane-trees on the Promenade / a ragamuffin enclave / carries on its raucous rural life / regardless! / Rooks... / rearing their young / on tottering airy rafts; / heedlessly dropping feathers, sticks / (and worse than sticks!) / on the prim pavements; / filling the seemly air with strident exclamation; flying and foraging / as if the smart and fashionable town / were still a village street / with new-ploughed fields and Cotswold sheep / only a step away.'

🦶 Proceed along The Promenade, passing Imperial Gardens (10) on your left.

★ Imperial Gardens
Originally created as pleasure gardens for subscribers to the Sherborne or Imperial Spa (see walk 2), today the gardens are filled each year with approximately 25,000 bedding plants. These provide magnificent floral displays, which are enjoyed by the many thousands of visitors who attend the outdoor events and festivals that take place here.

🦶 Continue along Montpellier Walk and enter Montpellier Gardens (11) on the left.

★ Montpellier Gardens
Montpellier Gardens were developed shortly after the opening of Montpellier Spa (see walk 2) in 1809. Again, originally conceived as exclusive pleasure gardens for visitors to the spa, tree-lined drives were soon constructed around the edge of the gardens for the fashionable society to enjoy when promenading.

🦶 Follow the path to the centre of the gardens. You can stop here for a drink at the Garden Café.
On your right you'll see a 200-year-old copper beech that dates from the original development of the gardens. Unfortunately it has now succumbed to a serious fungus, and eventually the 23-metre-tall tree will have to be removed, a sad loss to the town's environment, especially when one considers that this specimen is able to produce, in just one year, sufficient oxygen for more than ten people. However, the borough council has an active programme to replace old or diseased trees, and its mini-arboretum on the north-west side of Montpellier Gardens provides visible proof of this commitment.
🦶 Turn right along the path back towards Montpellier Walk. Turn left and, at the roundabout, take the third exit. Then turn left into Lypiatt Road (12).

★ Lypiatt Road

The link with the town's rural past is discernible through the word 'lypiatt', which means 'gate in an enclosure fence which only deer can leap'. Lypiatt Road, which had been developed by 1820 as part of the Suffolk estate, was originally built on a field called The Lypiatts. It was first laid out with elms, but now its street plantings have given way to garden and street trees which include silver birch, holm oak, horse chestnut, beech, yew and deodar cedar.

Turn right into Suffolk Road. You can stop at The Tivoli (34 Andover Road) for something to eat or drink.
Turn left into Tivoli Circus and proceed along Tivoli Road (13).

★ Tivoli Road

Tivoli Road is considered by many to be among Cheltenham's finest streets on account of its varied architecture and gardens. These gardens are filled with mature trees which include beech and pine, as well as a cut-leaved beech (*Fagus sylvatica var. heterophylla 'Asplenifolia'*). Many of the house fronts feature a central porch with large windows on either side surmounted by a curved recess, a design created by the famous London architect J. B. Papworth (1775–1847). Of particular interest is St Oswalds, a villa of around 1830–4 built in the 'Strawberry Hill Gothic' style and full of romantic extravagance. It is also worth noticing the blue plaque on No. 11, which records it as the birthplace of the actor Sir Ralph Richardson (1902–83), who always maintained close connections with Cheltenham, including when he opened the first literary festival in 1949. The Richardson Studio at the Everyman Theatre in Regent Street was

The chestnut tree (on left) that Ralph Richardson climbed as a boy.

named after him. He once commented, 'Whenever Cheltenham crops up in conversation I say with over-elaborate carelessness "As a matter of fact, I was born there" as if I owned the place.' Also of interest is the fact that the horse chestnut tree which he climbed as a boy and from which he called out to passers-by, 'How are you feeling today?' still stands today.

🐾 Turn right into The Park, then left through the main entrance of the university's Park Campus (14).

★ The Park
Located on the right of the car park is an interpretation panel identifying trees of special interest and marking out a circular route around the ornamental lake that is well worth following. Today, The Park estate is a community green space and a fine example of '*rus in urbe*', owned by the University of Gloucestershire in partnership with the Gloucestershire Wildlife Trust. However, in the 1830s it was at the centre of an ambitious plan to develop the Gloucestershire Zoological, Botanical and Horticultural Gardens. The venture soon failed and the exotic exhibits, including polar bears, kangaroos, monkeys and pelicans had to be sold off at the town's Assembly Rooms. The Park is now home to more than 900 trees, and the attractively laid-out grounds still provide reminders of its previous incarnation, not only in the ornamental lake designed in the shape of Africa, but also in the main walkway known as Elephant Walk, and the Italian-style Cornerways building with its striking tower, previously known as The Park Spa, which was the original entrance to the zoo. In the early 1840s the grounds were redeveloped as public pleasure grounds known as Park Gardens, an entry of one shilling being charged at Fullwood Lodge. Some of the mature specimens date from this time, including Corsican pine (planted *c.* 1849), false acacia (planted *c.* 1869–89), London plane (planted *c.* 1879) and giant redwood (planted *c.* 1889). Other notable specimens include the dawn redwood from China, which is critically endangered in the wild and sometimes described as a 'living fossil', as well as Monterey cypress, Austrian and Bhutan pine, blue atlas cedar, deodar, mulberry, sweet chestnut, yew, and tree of heaven.

🐾 Exit the campus via the main entrance. Turn left along The Park, then right into St Stephen's Road and left into Hatherley Court Road.

★ Hatherley Park
On your left, directly opposite Westal Park, you'll find the entrance to Hatherley Park (**15**). Hatherley Park was opened in 1939, having been redeveloped from land which previously formed part of Hatherley Court Estate. An interpretation panel situated by the ornamental lake gives background information and location details for thirteen different species of tree. These include 'living fossil' specimens such as the monkey puzzle tree or Chilean pine (*Araucaria araucana*), the maidenhair tree (*Gingko biloba*) and the dawn redwood (*Metasequoia glyptostroboides*), which was once thought to be extinct but was rediscovered in China in 1946. Other notable specimens include the Norway spruce (*Picea abies*), the deodar cedar (*Cedrus deodara*), the blue Atlantic cedar (*Cedrus atlantica glauca*), the hybrid black poplar, and the tulip tree (*Liriodendron tulipifera*), which was introduced to Britain in the reign of King Charles I. Water-loving trees are represented through the willow, oriental

plane (*Platanus orientalis*) and the alder, while native species such as oak are also present. Hatherley Park featured as one of the locations in Cheltenham where the 1979–83 BBC TV comedy series *Butterflies* was shot. Wendy Craig, who played the disillusioned 'stay-at-home' housewife, was frequently shown visiting the park and daydreaming on a bench overlooking the lake.

👣 **Return to the entrance of The Park campus. Then continue to the end of The Park. Turn left into Park Place, then immediately right into Grafton Road.**
This attractive avenue is lined with mature sycamores, horse chestnuts, a London plane and a beech.
👣 **Turn left into Bath Road and proceed to the entrance of Cheltenham College (16) on your right.**

★ Cheltenham College
Here, in front of the entrance to the college, is a smooth Arizona cypress (*Cupressus arizonica var. glabra*), one of only six local trees that are included in the *National Tree Register*. Located very close to the road, this attractive tree, with its bluish foliage, small, rounded cones and rich

Above left: Detail from the Unwin Fountain, Sandford Park.

Above right: Detail from the entrance gates to Pittville Park.

brown bark that peels in flakes, probably dates back to the time when the college was built in 1841. It measures 19 metres in height.

🐾 **Turn right into Sandford Road. Cross over and turn left into College Road.**
As you do so, notice the fine limes and, on the southern side, poplars that surround the college playing field. These form an important part of the college's cricketing heritage. Plaques beneath each tree indicate that they were planted to commemorate outstanding innings and bowling displays made by Old Cheltonians. Appropriately, trees and cricket played an important part in one of Cheltenham's most famous poems. When John Betjeman wrote his 'Cheltenham' poem while watching the Cricket Festival at the college ground, he remarked that he 'composed those lines when a summer wind / Was blowing the elm leaves dry'. However, by the end of the poem it is the limes that have the last word; Betjeman describes that 'behind the limes / Lengthens the Promenade'.
🐾 **Continue along College Road and turn left into Sandford Park (17).**

★ Sandford Park
Originally acquired by the borough council in 1927, the park was designed by the landscape architect Milner White. The name Sandford is derived from the 'sandy ford', which was once used to cross the River Chelt. Notice in particular the attractive fountain named after the Unwin family of Arle Court, now Cheltenham Film Studios, which is surrounded by a lovely group of rowans.

🐾 **Exit the park via the High Street entrance by turning right just before Barrat's Mill Lane.**
Here you will pass through the attractive Annecy Gardens, so named after one of Cheltenham's twin towns and adorned with pergolas and a lion-headed fountain. Since 2012 the gardens have been transformed into an edible garden by a local gardening group.
🐾 **There are several places to stop on the High Street for food and drink, including at Sandford Park Alehouse (20 High Street).**
🐾 **Turn left into the High Street, and then right into Winchcombe Street.**
At the end of this street you'll see the entrance gates to Pittville Park.
🐾 **Continue into Pittville Lawn and return to Pittville Pump Room.**

Walk 9

Theme and Variations

Distance: 2.7 miles
Minimum Time: 2 hours 30 mins
Parking: Chester Walk car park is most convenient.
Where to Eat and Drink: At the start/end of walk you can visit the Costa café at 33–41 The Promenade, where the artist Hamlet Millet once lived, or visit The Wilson Café at the Art Gallery & Museum in Clarence Street. Also, there are many fine cafés, bars and restaurants in the Montpellier Walk and High Street sections of the walk.
Where to stay: The Strozzi Palace (Tel. 01242 650028, www.strozzipalace.co.uk/cheltenham-boutique-hotel.php) at 55 St George's Place provides Italian inspiration in the form of a historic electricity substation modelled on Florence's Villa Strozzi. Another conveniently located guesthouse is Hanover House at 65 St George's Road (Tel 01242 541297, www.hanoverhouse.org), which contains many interesting works of art.

The *Theme and Variations* sculpture by Barbara Hepworth.

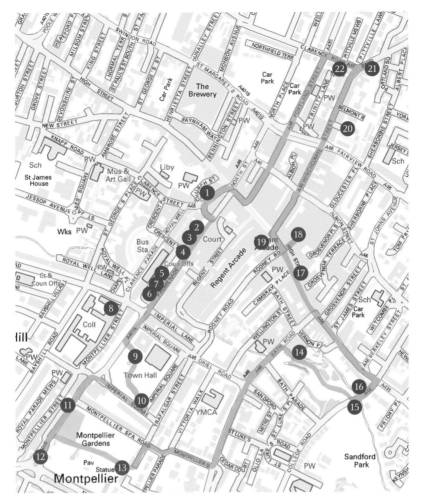

1. Cheltenham House
2. *The Minotaur and the Hare*
3. 33–41 The Promenade
4. Boer War memorial
5. 79 The Promenade
6. Neptune Fountain
7. Edward Wilson statue
8. Statue of lady holding an anchor
9. Gustav Holst statue
10. Imperial Fountain
11. The caryatids
12. Edward VII statue
13. William IV statue
14. *The Friendship Circle*
15. *The Weathered Man*
16. Stirling Court
17. Elephant Mural
18. Brian Jones bust
19. Wishing Fish Clock
20. *Man with Ball*
21. 21 Prestbury Road
22. Holst Birthplace Museum

In 1969, Barbara Hepworth (1903–75) was one of a select group of sculptors who were invited to consider a commission for the new headquarters building of the Cheltenham & Gloucester Building Society in the centre of Cheltenham. In the mid-1960s, much of Hepworth's work had been characterised by square shapes, but for this commission she chose a design based on a pattern of semicircular overlapping panels of bronze, which she called *Theme and Variations*. Measuring 11 feet in height by 25 feet in width, the mural sculpture still adorns the façade of Cheltenham House, which today is occupied by various shops and offices. It has been thought that the sculpture, with its shapes of differing sizes fanning out in three different configurations, creates the illusion of the gentle rocking movement of ships, inspired perhaps by the abstract paintings of boats in St Ives harbour by Terry Frost (1915–2003). But such an allusion is probably lost on many of those rushing along the Clarence Street section of the town's busy one-way traffic system.

Hepworth once said that she never began her work with a title, but always added it later, after she'd made something and could consider 'Where did I get that idea from?' Having mapped out this walk, aimed at exploring Cheltenham's rich artistic heritage, Hepworth's title of *Theme and Variations* seems particularly apposite. While there is an underlying, unifying 'theme' that links many of Cheltenham's public artworks – particularly, the collection of sculptures that bring together elements of the town's grand imperial or regal past – there is also an eclectic mix of new 'variations' that illustrates some of the changes that the town has grasped over recent decades, epitomised perhaps most prominently by *The Minotaur and the Hare* sculpture, which now stands centrestage in The Promenade. In previous times such controversial figures would not have been allowed entry to Cheltenham's most exclusive thoroughfare; the police constables who once stood guard at the entrance would have allowed only members of the gentry to gain entry.

👣 **The walk starts at Cheltenham House (1), Clarence Street, the location of *Theme and Variations*.**
A visit should be made to The Wilson at the beginning or end of the walk to visit its extensive collections, including its internationally renowned Arts & Crafts collection.
👣 **Turn right into Imperial Circus and then right into The Promenade.**

★ *The Minotaur and the Hare*
Opposite Cavendish House you'll find the 10-foot-high sculpture entitled *The Minotaur and the Hare* (**2**), which was created by Sophie Ryder in 1995. When it was first located in the lower Promenade it aroused considerable controversy, journalists delighting prematurely in

The Minotaur and the Hare sculpture on The Promenade.

the pun 'Hare today, gone tomorrow'. The town became divided between those who wanted to keep the bronze figures as a permanent installation and those who considered that it was not suited to the Regency architecture. Despite this, its supporters raised £50,000 through public subscription to acquire the sculpture in 1998. Today, it has not only become an important meeting place and minor attraction, but was also made the subject of a new local play in 2013. Sophie Ryder once commented, 'I prefer that people read their own stories into the works. So although the figures are 100 per cent human, they are disguised by their masks.'

★ Hamlet Millet
Directly behind the sculpture at 33–41 The Promenade is the building (**3**), now occupied by Waterstone's, that was originally built in 1823 as the home of the artist Hamlet Millet (*c.* 1768–1852). Millet was an acquaintance of Lord Byron and one of the most successful miniature portrait painters of his day. The building later became the Imperial Hotel, and then the Imperial Club, which was open only to 'resident noblemen and gentlemen', and then finally served as Cheltenham's main post office from 1874 until 1987 before it was converted into a shop.

Continue to 79 The Promenade (5) on the right-hand side.
As you walk there, notice on your left the striking Boer War Memorial (**4**), which commemorates the men of Cheltenham who died in the South African war of 1899–1902.

★ Hugo van Wadenoyen
As the blue plaque on 79 The Promenade records, it was here that the photographer Hugo van Wadenoyen (1892–1959) had his studio between 1936 and 1956. Of Dutch descent, Hugo settled in Cheltenham in the early 1930s and quickly established a reputation for high-quality artistic photography, excelling particularly in informal portraits of children, which were in stark contrast to the prevailing formal approaches of the day. Standing 6 feet tall, and with a camera always around his neck, his lean and slightly stooped frame made him a well-known figure along The Promenade. However, his influence was far from parochial. An avid promoter of photography as an art form, he conveyed pioneering ideas about portraiture and landscape photography through frequent lectures, radio broadcasts and books, among which *Photographing People: Ways to New Portraiture* (1939) and *Wayside Snapshots* (1947) were seminal works. One of his most influential ideas was to reject 'pictorialism' in landscape photography, and advocate direct realism instead of the prevailing approach of making photographs look like engravings. Although sometimes regarded as a loner, Hugo counted the artist John Piper (1903–92) who regularly came to visit him in Cheltenham as one of his close friends. Also, among his many admirers was John Betjeman, who once wrote to Cecil Beaton to say that Hugo was very much 'my type [of photographer]'. Examples of his local work can be seen at the Local and Family History Centre as well as The Wilson, where there is also a portrait of him by Rhoda Elliott (1902–83).

Continue to the Neptune Fountain (6), passing the Edward Wilson statue (7) (see walk 6) on your left.

★ Neptune Fountain
This ornate sculpture (see also walk 1), based on the Trevi Fountain in Rome, was designed

by the borough engineer Joseph Hall, and shows Neptune, the Roman god of the sea, with sea horses and tritons. It was carved in 1893 and once formed a feature in front of the Imperial Spa (see walk 2), which was demolished in 1937. Previously, the fountain was surrounded by a weeping willow, grown from a cutting of a tree on St Helena, which was one of Napoleon's favourites.

🦶 **Turn right into St George's Road.**
On your left, notice the statue of a lady holding an anchor (**8**) on the façade at about the second-floor level of the Ladies' College building. Symbolising Hope, this was designed by H. H. Martyn (see below). When Martyn was informed by an admiral who lived in the area that the anchor was wrongly shaped, he had it recarved.
🦶 **Return to The Promenade and turn right. Then take the first path on the left to enter Imperial Gardens.**
Observe the statue of Gustav Holst (**9**) (see walk 7) from close up.
🦶 **Then continue diagonally across the gardens. Cross the road towards the corner of the square.**
Next to No. 37, you'll see an impressive marble fountain (**10**) tucked back into an alcove of the building.

★ **Imperial Fountain**
Also known as the Napoleon Fountain, in 1800 the Imperial Fountain was first looted by the French from Italy, only to be captured by the British while being conveyed to France. It was subsequently sold to Thomas Henney, a Cheltenham solicitor, who installed it in 1826 near the Imperial Spa (see walk 2), now the site of the Queen's Hotel.

🦶 **Turn to face Imperial Gardens, turn left along the square towards The Promenade with the Queen's Hotel on the left. Cross the road towards Queen's Circus, before turning left onto Montpellier Walk to see the caryatids (11) on your right.**

★ **Caryatids**
There are thirty-two caryatids in total, acting as supporting columns for the lintels of the shop façades. Two of these figures of armless Grecian virgins, based on the models at the Erechtheion in Athens, date from 1840 and were made by the London sculptor Henry Rossi from terracotta. The rest are copies in stone produced in 1970 by a local stonemason called James Brown. In 1978, the poet Adrian Mitchell (1932–2008) was engaged as guest writer at the literature festival, during which he produced 'a six-day book' of impressions about the town entitled *Naked in Cheltenham or the Music will Never Stop*. One of the most memorable pieces in this is his encounter with the caryatids, which, he notices, 'differ slightly, but not on purpose'. Describing each one individually, as 'glum', 'vacant', 'dominant', 'timid', 'smooth', appearing to whistle, or having a defect such as a dented nose, he concludes that he'd like to return to a future literature festival so that he could give each one a name: 'After all,' he writes, 'even the Seven Dwarfs had names.'

🦶 **You can stop to eat and drink at numerous cafés, bars and restaurants such as John**

The caryatids, Montpellier Walk.

Gordon's (11 Montpellier Arcade) or Gusto Italian Deli and Caffe (12 Montpellier Walk).
Continue up Montpellier Walk to the Rotunda on your right.

On your left, in the middle of the road, is a statue of Edward VII (**12**), which Adrian Mitchell mistakes for Winston Churchill 'because of the way he holds his head, like a bull'.

★ Edward VII

In fact, the statue shows King Edward VII dressed in a Norfolk suit, a style he popularised, offering benevolence to a barefoot waif. Originally unveiled in 1914, it was donated by Mr and Mrs Drew of Hatherley Court, who were known for rescuing retired horses and donkeys. The statue incorporates a drinking fountain below, which was originally provided for carriage horses.

Cross the road towards Montpellier Gardens, then follow the fence down to the left before turning right into the gardens.

★ William IV

At the end of the path there is a rare statue of King William IV (**13**), one of only two in existence. It depicts the king in robes and was erected to mark the passing of the Reform Bill in 1833, which made provision for Cheltenham to have a Member of Parliament. Originally sited in Imperial Gardens, it was moved to Montpellier Gardens in 1920.

Turn left in front of the statue, then right into Montpellier Spa Road. Follow the road round to the left then turn right into Montpellier Drive. Turn left into Bath Road and then

Statue of William IV, Montpellier Gardens.

after 200 metres turn right through the entrance into Sandford Park. Follow the path over the bridge and straight on to the *Friendship Circle* (14).

★ *Friendship Circle*

Created in 1993 by the South African-born artist Neville Gabie (b. 1959), this set of shell-like sculptures in cast iron was one of the first council-funded art installations in Cheltenham, and symbolises the twinning of Cheltenham with other towns, such as Annecy in France, Göttingen in Germany, and Cheltenham Township in Pennsylvania USA, a place that even shares the same crest.

👣 Continue straight on and exit the park by turning left into College Road.

Notice the sculpture called *The Weathered Man* (15) (see walk 1) on your right in the park opposite, lying in a prone position.

★ H. H. Martyn

On your left, at the corner of College Road and High Street, you'll see Stirling Court (16). This was the site of the premises once used by the architectural craftsman and philanthropist Herbert Henry Martyn (1842–1937). The company formed by H. H. Martyn found worldwide recognition through its production of high-quality wood, stone and metal carvings for buildings such as St Paul's Cathedral, Buckingham Palace and the House of Commons. In Cheltenham it produced carvings of unrivalled excellence for Cheltenham College, the Ladies' College and some local churches. However, Martyn's fame was also built on his philanthropic nature, which saw him develop a mission for the poor in Cheltenham as well as a temperance society and a working men's college.

👣 Turn left into the High Street. You can stop to eat and drink at numerous cafés, bars and restaurants such as Café Moochoo (51 High Street) or The Strand (42 High Street). After several hundred metres turn right into Grosvenor Place South opposite Cambray Place.

★ Elephant Mural

On your right in the alleyway you'll see a set of five mosaic panels (17), comprising over 90,000 pieces, which were created by Turton and Robertson in 1993 to celebrate an unusual but true event of 1934, when three elephants from a travelling circus went on the rampage in Cheltenham as bystanders looked on with both alarm and delight. An article from the *Gloucestershire Echo* of 26 March 1934 recorded it thus:

Three elephants from Chapman's London Zoo Circus were passing with two keepers along Albion-street, Cheltenham at lunch time today when opposite the shop of Bloodworth and Sons, seed merchants, a small stampede occurred, and one elephant finally entered the shop and another got half inside. Even an elephant likes a change of diet, and Jumbo can be decidedly awkward when he plans to vary the menu himself. Mr W. T. Goodhall, manager of the shop was attending to his books when he heard shouting. Looking up he saw a giant shape shambling through the doorway. Imagine his surprise when, with mind calmly engrossed with pounds, shillings and pence, in walks an elephant and without so much as a by your leave, helps itself to seed potatoes, dog biscuits, meal and other elephantine luxuries. One of the keepers was unable to get in to the shop until the elephant, which completely filled the threshold, had entered. Once inside the keeper set about forcibly changing the elephant's mind. His task was made more difficult for another elephant was already half way through the door. The other, still in the road, was being kept under control, and after about five minutes of belabouring the intruders were evicted. Fortunately very little damage was done, and Mr Goodhall and his assistant, after gathering up the potatoes, and putting the shop straight, were able to realise the humour of the situation.

The Friendship Circle sculptures, Sandford Park.

AMAZED CHELTONIANS AND THE
LOCAL CONSTABULARY WATCHED WITH
ALARM AND DELIGHT.

One of the panels from the Elephant Mural.

The five panels summarise each section of the story in the following way: 'The Circus parade begins to work its way through town'; 'The Ringmaster advertises the Circus'; 'One of the Elephants breaks free and heads for the goodies'; 'A keeper struggles to remove one of the Elephants'; and 'The police and locals look on aghast'. It is not known whether this event was a chance occurrence or a deliberate act on the part of the circus owners to attract publicity.

🐾 **Continue down the High Street to the entrance of the Beechwood Shopping Centre.**
A short detour from here may be made to see the bust of Rolling Stones 'golden boy' Brian Jones (1942–69) (**18**), which is located near the water feature in the centre of the arcade.

★ **Brian Jones**
Jones was born in Cheltenham, attended both Dean Close Preparatory and Pate's Grammar schools, and played with many Cheltenham-based bands before placing an advert to start the Rolling Stones rock group, the name being derived from a Muddy Waters song. His funeral was held at Cheltenham Minster after he tragically drowned under mysterious circumstances in a swimming pool, and he is buried at Cheltenham cemetery in Bouncers Lane.

🐾 **Continue down the High Street and turn left into the Regent Arcade.**

★ **Wishing Fish Clock**
Inside the arcade, suspended over the main walkway, you'll see the 45-foot-tall, 3-ton wishing fish clock (**19**), which was designed by artist and author Kit Williams (b. 1946) and built by Cheltenham clockmakers Sinclair Harding & Co. Unveiled in 1987, it is reputed to be the world's tallest mechanical clock. The features of the clock include a white duck that lays a never-ending supply of golden eggs, carried down in red egg cups; a family of mice that is constantly trying to evade the attention of a hunting snake, and a huge fish, which blows bubbles every half hour to the tune of 'I'm forever blowing bubbles.' Make a wish if you catch one of the bubbles!

On your way you'll pass a commemorative model in a glass case of the first jet engine, which was designed by Sir Frank Whittle (1907–96) and assembled in a garage previously located on this site.

🐾 **Return to the High Street. Turn right and then left into Winchcombe Street. Cross Albion Street and then Fairview Road.**
Set back from the junction with Sheldon's Court on your right is a bronze statue by Giles Penny (b. 1962) called *Man with Ball* (**20**).

★ *Man with Ball*
This sculpture was commissioned in 2000 by Crest Homes Ltd as the centrepiece for their housing development in Regency Mews. Penny, who originally trained in formal painting, often initiates his ideas for sculptures in painting or lithography and then transforms them into abstracted versions of the human form, which he uses to convey emotions and feelings, often with 'an innocent humorous quality'.

The wishing fish clock in the Regent Arcade.

🐾 **Continue on and pass near the entrance gates to Pittville Park. Then turn right to 21 Prestbury Road (21).**

Here you'll find a blue plaque commemorating the birthplace of the artist Hector Caffieri (1847–1932). In fact, the plaque looks more associated with No. 23, but in any case it has been wrongly sited since Hector was born at 3 Portland Place, in a house located on what is today currently occupied by the North Road car park, now under redevelopment. The son of a wine merchant who traded in Montpellier Walk, Caffieri went on to study art in Paris under the tutelage of Léon Bonnat (1833–1922) and Jules-Joseph Lefebvre (1836–1911), and achieved recognition as a prolific artist, specialising particularly in landscapes, coastal scenes and still life. A fine example of his work, entitled *Boulogne Harbour*, forms part of the collection of paintings in The Wilson.

🐾 **Turn back along Prestbury Road and turn right into Clarence Road.**

★ **Theodor von Holst**

On your left, at No. 4, you'll come to the Holst Birthplace Museum (**22**) (see also walk 7). Here you can explore the artistic legacy of Gustav Holst's younger brother, Theodor von Holst (1810–44). Although Theodor died at just thirty-three years of age, his collection of work later exerted considerable influence on an important movement in nineteenth-century art known as the Pre-Raphaelite Brotherhood. He also achieved considerable success as an illustrator, and is not only considered as one of the most important illustrators of German Romantic literature, but also has the distinction of being the first to illustrate Mary Shelley's *Frankenstein; or, The Modern Prometheus* (1818).

🐾 **Continue along Clarence Road, then turn left into Portland Street and continue on as it joins Pittville Street.**

Just before the junction with Albion Street notice the magnificent Masonic hall (see walk 8) on your right.

🐾 **Turn right into the High Street and, at Boots Corner, turn left into Clarence Street to return to the start of the walk.**

The walk finishes here. However, there are several other sites within the town which are well worth visiting, including the striking artwork entitled *Barley* by Sophie Marsham, which stands at the entrance to the Brewery complex; the *Listening Stones* in Hester's Way Park, located near GCHQ, which has been dubbed 'Cheltenham's Stonehenge', comprising nine glacial granite boulders covered with various codes and ciphers, reflecting the theme of communications and celebrating GCHQ's move to its 'doughnut' building; and the range of art installations and sculptures at Cheltenham Racecourse, which includes statues of Arkle, Golden Miller and Best Mate as well as a life-size bust of HRH The Queen Mother.

Acknowledgements

I am most grateful to Nicola Gale at Amberley for commissioning the book. Also, a number of organisations, societies, museums, libraries and archive services have provided me with excellent support. My thanks in particular go to all the staff at Cheltenham Reference and Local History Libraries, Ann-Rachael Harwood at The Wilson, Cheltenham's Art Gallery & Museum, Christine Leighton and Jill Barlow at Cheltenham College Archives, and Laura Kinnear at the Holst Birthplace Museum. I am also grateful to the following for making many helpful suggestions, including testing out the walks, sometimes in inclement weather: Steve Blake, Chris Chavasse, Margaret Eccles, Roger Graham, Mark and Rosemary Hartley, Mick Kippin, Cherry Lavell, Graham Lockwood, Katherine MacInnes, Lindsey Mulraine, James and Veronica Ritchie, Derek Rowles and Anne Strathie. My heartfelt thanks go to my family, Meg, Rachel and Catrin, for their patience, support and encouragement.

I am most grateful to the following for granting me kind permission to reproduce the following copyright material: 'Bird's Eye View' © John Betjeman by permission of The Estate of John Betjeman; extract from 'Spring Day, Cheltenham', in *Gloucestershire Pieces*, © Sheila Simmons 1983. Extract from 'How the trees came to Cheltenham' is reproduced from *Tree Music*, © Lady Margaret Sackville 1947. Extracts from 'In praise of walking' are reproduced from Distance and Proximity, © Thomas A. Clark 2000. All images are © the Author. The maps included in this book contain Ordnance Survey data © Crown copyright and database right 2011.